To God and family and friends,
and to the athletes
of time and the world:
you lead us to reach beyond our grasp
and we are better for your example.

SPORTS
AND
ATHLETICS

Joseph C. Mihalich is a professor of philosophy and former department chairman at La Salle College in Philadelphia, PA, and represented the college as a faculty delegate at NCAA national conventions. He is a member of the constitution revision committee of the Philosophic Society for the Study of Sport, and is an active member of the National Academic Athletic Advisors Association.

Dr. Mihalich received his B.A. (Journalism) and M.A. (Social Philosophy) degrees from Duquesne University in Pittsburgh, PA. He studied in the Licentiate in Philosophy program at The Catholic University of America in Washington, D.C., before receiving his Ph.D. in philosophy from Georgetown University in Washington. He also played professional baseball in the Chicago Cubs, (Brooklyn) Dodgers, and New York Yankee organizations.

SPORTS
AND
ATHLETICS

PHILOSOPHY
IN ACTION

Joseph C. Mihalich

1982
LITTLEFIELD, ADAMS & COMPANY

Copyright © 1982 by
LITTLEFIELD, ADAMS & CO.
81 Adams Drive, Totowa, N.J. 07512

Library of Congress Cataloging in Publication Data

Mihalich, Joseph C.
  Sports and athletics.

  (Littlefield, Adams quality paperback)
  Includes bibliographical references.
  1. Sports—Philosophy. 2. Athletics—Philosophy.
I. Title.
GV706.M52   796'.01   81-20837
ISBN O-8226-0371-3 (pbk.)   AACR2

Printed in the United States of America

Contents

Preface

This book is inspired by Paul Weiss and Michael Novak, whose writings articulate Plato's adage (in *Laws*) that we are "created as a plaything of the gods, and that is the best part of us." Scholarly interest in the philosophical and humanistic aspects of sports and athletics has increased significantly in recent decades, and it is gratifying that we have come even so lately to appreciate the importance of *ludens* in *sapiens*.'

Prefaces usually include acknowledgments to people and institutions "who make this book possible," and a few such references are in order here. My friend Paul Cronin read and critiqued (with wit and intelligence) more versions of this manuscript than either of us cares to remember, and my wife Dolores provided more literary and spiritual help than we thought would be needed. John Wieboldt directed this project with benevolence and enthusiasm, and Sally Held's editorial guidance accounts for its professional character. The greatest collective contribution comes from my philosophy students over the years, who have taught me to appreciate the human dimension in the educational experience.

A sincere acknowledgment is extended to Emery C. Mollenhauer, F.S.C., Provost of La Salle College, Philadelphia, PA, and to the college administration for providing the scholar's ultimate luxury: financed free time for labors of love. This confidence and support from respected colleagues is "the best part" of what follows.

Acknowledgments

Grateful appreciation is extended to the following for permission to reprint selected material from the specified publications.

Basic Books, Inc., *Publishers,* and Michael Novak, from *The Joy of Sports: End Zones, Bases, Baskets, Balls, and the Consecration of the American Spirit* by Michael Novak. (c) 1976 by Michael Novak. Published by Basic Books, Inc., New York. Reprinted by permission.

Bradley, Senator William Warren, N.J., from "You Can't Buy Heart" by Bill Bradley, *Sports Illustrated,* Time Inc., New York, 31 October 1977.

Charles C. Thomas, Publisher, from *The Philosophy of Sport: A Collection of Original Essays* ed. Robert G. Osterhoudt, 1973. Courtesy of Charles C. Thomas, Publisher, Springfield, Illinois.

Doubleday and Company, Garden City, New York, and Routledge & Kegan Paul Ltd., London, from *Man in the Modern Age* by Karl Jaspers, 1952.

Harper & Row, Publishers, Inc., New York, from *Dynamics of Faith* by Paul Tillich. Reprinted by permission of Harper & Row, Publishers, Inc.

Human Kinetics Publishers, Champaign, Illinois, from *Joy and Sadness in Children's Sports* by Rainer Martens, 1978.

MacMillan Publishing Co., New York, from *Man, Play and Games* by Roger Caillois. Copyright (c) 1961 by The Free Press.

McCarthy, Dr. Thomas, N., La Salle College, Philadelphia, PA, from policy address on intercollegiate athletics, December 1976.

Messenger Press, Celina, Ohio, from "Man and Sport" by Keith Algozin, *Philosophy Today*, Fall 1976.

Mollenhauer, Emery C., F.S.C., Provost, La Salle College, Philadelphia, PA, from La Salle College Self-Study Report, 1975.

Phi Delta Kappan, Bloomington, Indiana, from "College Football and Mr. Chips: All in the Family" by Robert T. Blackburn and Michael S. Nyikos, October 1974; and from "Student-Athletes: Tackling the Problem" by Bob Hammell (panel moderator); also related articles by Stephen Horn and John M. Stevens, September 1980.

Philosophical Library, New York, from *Being and Nothingness* by Jean-Paul Sartre, trans. Hazel E. Barnes, Philosophical Library, New York, 1956.

Random House, Inc., New York, from *Sports in America* by James A. Michener. Copyright (c) 1976 by Random House Inc.

Southern Illinois University Press, Carbondale, Illinois, from *Sport: A Philosophic Inquiry* by Paul Weiss. Copyright (c) 1969 by Southern Illinois University Press. Reprinted by permission of Southern Illinois University Press.

The New York Times, from "Athletic Scholarships Yes — Academic Scholarships No" by Dr. George Sheehan, 10 November 1974; and from "University of Southern California Self-Study Report" 19 October 1980. (c) 1974/1980 by *The New York Times Co.*

The Philadelphia Inquirer, and Sandra Kohler, from "Sports and the Arts are Compatible" by Sandra Kohler, 11 January 1978, *The Philadelphia Inquirer*, Philadelphia, Pennsylvania.

Ziff-Davis Publishing Co., New York, from "Sport is a Western Yoga" by Adam Smith. Reprinted from *Psychology Today Magazine*. Copyright 1975 Ziff-Davis Publishing Co.

INTRODUCTION

Confronting the Issues

At one point in his playing days with the New York Yankees, the legendary Yogi Berra was in a batting slump presumably aggravated by his well-known tendency to swing at pitches out of the strike zone. He sought help from the team's hitting instructor, who promptly advised him that "You've got to think up there at the plate—don't just swing at anything." In his droll and laconic manner, Yogi replied, "I can't think and hit at the same time—it's got to be one or the other."

This is a book about thinking and hitting and about thought and action and sports and athletics as causal forces in what we are and what we strive to be. Contrary to public and professional opinion, sports and athletics are much more than fun and games, and more than mere entertainment for the sports fans of the world. Sports and athletics are philosophical and humanistic dimensions in human existence and contribute significantly to the meaning of mankind and the shaping of civilization. Along with our unique capacities for knowledge, love, and aesthetic fulfillment, the sporting experience is an essential and definitive factor in human nature. Where there are people, where there is any form of social or cultural organization, there will be the inevitable expression of the sporting spirit.

Philosophical treatises have described sports and athletics as the greatest opportunity for the achievement of human excellence and the most universal social context for developing cherished values, including courage, honesty, freedom, discipline, and communal effort. The sporting experience serves as a paradigm in serious philosophical analyses on such issues as the nature of ethics and morality, the content of aesthetic productivity, and the substance of religious convictions. Play-forms and game principles, the structural context of sports and athletics, are cited in scholarly studies on the ideological foundations of society and culture. The ultimate symbolism of life and death is reflected metaphorically in the "joy of victory and the agony of defeat" in the sporting enterprise.

And yet relatively little has been written on the philosophy (and theology) of sports and athletics. We have numerous anecdotal accounts of athletic heroes and would-be heroes, and some valuable historical studies and accounts of records and statistics, but disproportionately few scholarly investigations of the philosophical and humanistic aspects of sports and athletics. This curious paradox of historical neglect extends even from the time of the early Greek philosophers, who were notably prolific and represented a society of celebrated concern with athletic prowess; yet they wrote of sports and athletics only briefly and in the context of other issues.

In the past several decades, however, serious academic research in the humanities of sports and athletics has increased without precedent and beyond anticipation, with the major impetus coming from a pioneer band of scholars in the Philosophic Society for the Study of Sport (PSSS). The society itself was founded only in 1972 (with eminent philosopher Paul Weiss as founding president) and functions now as an international organization dedicated to pedagogy and research in the philosophical and humanistic areas of the sporting enterprise.

This is a book about the philosophy of sports and athletics, with special reference to the importance of the sporting experience in the educational process and especially in higher education. What is presented here is the content of a college-level course on the philosophy of sports developed over a period of years with significant results in student appeal and academic respectability. With the use of audiovisual libraries and the recruitment of guest experts in specialty areas (such as sports medicine and sports law), this will serve as a primer text and reference source for a semester course in a typical college or university curriculum. Despite this pedagogical context or thrust, the popular nature of the subject matter and the familiarity of the discussions will appeal to the general reader as well.

Methods employed in this study are analytical and expository in nature and are intended to establish a reasoned, philosophical basis for understanding the integral character of sports and athletics in human existence and experience. If there is any specific ideological bias or prejudice reflected in these pages, it would be the merger of traditional philosophical attitudes with the personalism and individualism typified in existentialist philosophy. The philosophical conviction represented is that human nature has definitive goals and purposes applicable to all people, but these goals and purposes must be interpreted and fulfilled in personal experiences and individual expressions of humanity. These experiences and expressions are sometimes manifested in more esoteric pursuits, such as art, literature, and statesmanship, and sometimes in activities like sports and athletics. All such manifestations are equally valid and credible as personal testaments to the human spirit.

This book is written with sincere conviction born of personal experience and lifelong observation that sports and athletics make better people, enrich lives, and create more devoted families and resolute societies. More frequently than any other single segment of the human species, athletes portray, in brief shining moments, the highest ideals of dedicated striving and heroic accomplishment. There are forms and instances of dishonesty, exploitation, greed, and avarice in sports and athletics, just as there are in other human pursuits where hearts and minds compete seriously for signal acceptance and personal gain. Whether in sports and athletics, national politics and international statesmanship, or in commerce and industry, the sins of the human factor should never obscure the essential worth of the systems and institutions of human achievement. The potential for good in the sporting enterprise far outweighs the failures of the human flesh, and it is imperative for our present and future well-being as a species that the games should go on.

Great writers and serious minds throughout history have extolled the virtues and values of sports and athletics, beginning with the epic poet Homer and extending to the present day through scholars, cultural commentators, and sports figures. Critics have also existed and sometimes justifiably attack the excesses and defects in this typically human pursuit. Sports and athletics constitute a microcosm of society and thus tend to reflect the ills of an overly mercenary and commercial social structure. The contemporary sports world is flawed by the same moral deficiencies displayed in society at large: excessive emphasis on financial status as the measure of success; the "win at any cost syndrome" resulting in dishonesty and exploitation; excessive violence and aggression as a modus operandi; and illicit and medically questionable abuse of drugs and artificial stimulants. The ideal of decency and integrity in the sporting enterprise depends on similar standards in our social and cultural orientation.

Our intense involvement with sports and athletics derives from the dissolution of the Puritan ethic, or the work ethic, which contends that man is born to *work*, and play and games should, at best, be only tolerated. The dissolution of the work ethic (the beginning of mankind's freedom from total and constant involvement with manual labor) originates in the Industrial Revolution and culminates in our advanced technological civilization. Scientific innovations leading to increased material productivity have provided modern man with an unprecedented abundance of leisure time, with a concomitant increase in play activities as a legitimate expression of the human spirit.

Play and games (and sports and athletics) are defined in the larger context of work and leisure time, and the distinctions are sometimes subtle and subject to personal interpretations and value judgments. Especially in contemporary sports and athletics, the most troublesome distinction is the aspect of socioeconomic productivity and financial investments and returns. These are nominally aspects of the world of work and seriousness, and are anomalies in the free–spirited, spontaneous world of play and games and sports and athletics. The innovation is that contemporary sports programs are expansive business empires, and serious athletes are involved in work and play at the same time with corresponding rewards and experiences.

In *Sport: A Philosophic Inquiry*, probably the most definitive work in the philosophy of sports in recent literature, Paul Weiss argues that the sporting experience constitutes our greatest opportunity for the achievement and witnessing of human excellence. Human excellence naturally attracts us, and we pursue excellence in every form. Commonly recognized forms of human excellence in scholarly and spiritual contexts are restricted to relatively few and usually more mature people, while physical excellence in sports and athletics is possible for many more people and at a younger age. Serious sports participants actually pursue excellence, and sports spectators share vicariously in the revelation of what man can be and do when pushed to the limits of physical being.

This argument transcends in scope and applicability the commonly offered explanations for our timeless and universal fascination for sports and athletics. These explanations generally reduce to the contentions that the sporting experience (a) builds character and develops sound, virtuous human qualities; (b) contributes to our sense of social community and respect for others; (c) provides a means and an opportunity for fame and fortune; and (d) constitutes an acceptable outlet for violence and aggression. These answers are all true to some extent, but fall short of the complete rationale which must apply realistically to participants and also to spectators as an essential aspect of the sporting enterprise.

This philosophical view that sports and athletics produce human excellence makes it relatively easy to state the case for intercollegiate athletic programs. The main business of colleges and universities is to promote excellence in every form, and thus intercollegiate sports are an essential component of the college experience in theory and practice. Meaningful education is always education of the total person in mind and body. Academic administrators who think of sports and athletics as expendable afterthoughts or evil necessities are actually undermining the total educational process.

In a novel and probably controversial interpretation of the sporting enterprise, philosopher–sociologists Johan Huizinga and Roger Caillois (*Man, Play and Games*) assert that sports and athletics are involved in the very foundations of society and culture. The thesis is that play–forms and game principles reflected in the sporting experience actually shape and mold society and culture and constitute their ideological foundations. This reverses the popular assumption that play–forms and game principles (and sports and athletics) *derive* from given societies and cultures and exist as products of previously established social and cultural orientations.

The four basic game principles are *agon* (competition and struggle in games and in society); *alea* (the chance element in games and in society); *mimicry* (illusion and imitation in games and in society); and *ilinx* or *vertigo* (alterations in natural equilibrium in games and in society). These game principles are reflected in typical social contexts, such as competitive situations in business and industry; Wall Street speculation and state lotteries; theater, drama, and symbolic rituals; and attempts to change one's views of reality. These principles are good in themselves, but contain the potential for excesses which disrupt and corrupt society. It is surprising and disturbing to realize that game principles are the latent cause of some of our most serious social and cultural maladies: violence, deceit, and superstition; self–alienation and personality disorders; and alcoholism and drug addiction.

These game principles combine to form the foundation for the two major types of historical social development: the Apollonian culture or tradition, and the Dionysian culture or tradition. The Apollonian tradition is based on rationality and rules–governed forms of competition and chance and thus reflects the combination of *agon* and *alea* as social determinants. The Dionysian tradition is expressed in primitive and emotionally oriented social structures and thus projects the combination of *mimicry* and *ilinx* as social determinants. Our American society clearly indicates the Apollonian influence in our collective devotion to such *agon-alea* symbols as the World Series, the Rose Bowl, and the Stanley Cup playoffs.

One of the most specific philosophical expressions of the sporting experience occurs in existentialist philosophy, a popular contemporary attitude emphasizing the "primacy and dignity of the human reality as an individual in the world." Existentialism focuses on the *hard immediacy* of personal decisions as the context of knowledge and value. Existentialism in sports and athletics centers on the concept of the athlete as an individual in the world, as one who is intensely committed to personal values and goals for the moment and for one's athletic lifetime. The athlete as existentialist is measured by actions and deeds actually performed now and forever, and never by intentions that exist only in the realm of the abstract.

Some of the classic existentialist philosophers who have commented directly or indirectly on the significance of the sporting experience in human existence and experience are Soren Kierkegaard, Friedrich Nietzsche, Karl Jaspers, Jose Ortega y Gassett, Albert Camus, and Jean-Paul Sartre. Kierkegaard is concerned primarily with the nature of religious experience, but there are intriguing extensions in his thought that relate to sports and athletics. Nietzsche's emphasis on *play* as the symbol of human freedom and the good life climaxes in his famous figure of the "superman or overman or übermensch," and it is tempting to suggest that this heroic role is best expressed in the triumphs of the serious athlete.

Jean-Paul Sartre is generally recognized as the most authoritative spokesperson for the existentialist movement, and the central theme in his philosophy is absolute human freedom: "to be human is to be free and to be free is to be human." This is the theme he perceives clearly in play and games and sports and athletics, and this is the measure of the play world's reality and authenticity. Mankind committed to the serious work world is not free—only man at play is free to be creative and to establish rules and principles for authentic human existence. Sartre's views on play and sport emphasize that the play world is the *real* world—the world of what we are and what we should be.

An intriguing variation on existentialism's experiential (rather than conceptual) approach to sports and athletics is reflected in sporadic but enthusiastic accounts of Zen philosophies and other forms of Eastern mysticism applied to the sporting experience. This approach contends that properly oriented athletes can achieve surprisingly successful results by eliminating the "mind and ego–consciousness" from their physical performances and withdrawing into a mystical state in which the body is "let go" to function as an entity in itself. The very nature of this view of successful sports performances defies any extended logical analysis.

This book is concerned especially with intercollegiate sports and athletics, where so many aspects and interests tend to converge. College athletic programs are probably the most popular and controversial area in the contemporary sports scene, and vociferous debates are waged constantly about the nature and purpose of athletics in higher education. As in every other area of the sporting enterprise, intercollegiate sports and athletics have the positive potential to produce human excellence and also the disastrous potential for abuse and corruption. The latter is particularly disturbing in intercollegiate sports since it involves the betrayal of lofty educational ideals and sacred trusts ingrained in the guiding institutions of civilization.

Especially in this day and age of increasingly vocal criticism of intercollegiate athletic programs (some of it certainly justified), it is important to establish the rationale for sound and successful sports activities in our colleges and universities. Some critics of collegiate sports programs would take the quick and easy way by eliminating or thoroughly de-emphasizing such activities, but this would be a serious loss for society and would vitiate the purposes and goals of the educational process. There are various ways to explicate the rationale for sound and successful intercollegiate programs, including the pursuit of human excellence described in some detail above. Other related interpretations stress the benefits to the institution in terms of recruitment and retention of students and loyal (contributing) alumni and the general enhancement of the institution in public recognition. More specific aspects include special forms of motivation on the part of the student-athlete (self-knowledge and self-discipline), which frequently translate into greater personal and academic achievement.

Integrity and probity in intercollegiate sports and athletics begins with institutional responsibility in conducting ethically oriented programs for the benefit of everyone involved. Institutional responsibility is summarized in four important principles: (1) the need to recognize and emphasize the orientation of student–athletes as students first and athletes second; (2) the need to recognize in a reasonable and just way the unique physical and psychological pressures and unusual time–energy demands on serious student–athletes; (3) the need to recognize the mutually beneficial character of the institution's willingness to restrict privileges and considerations for student–athletes to National Collegiate Athletic Association (NCAA) and Association of Intercollegiate Athletics for Women (AIAW) regulations—and to what is available in principle to all students.

In many basic respects, the central figure in the controversy about intercollegiate athletics is the student–athlete. The plight of the serious student–athlete is easily depicted. Compared to nonathlete students, the student–athlete has two sets of responsibilities and obligations and two sets of goals and objectives. These combined academic/athletic requirements subject student–athletes to two sets of taskmasters vying for their undivided time and attention, two sets of priorities vying for their finite time and energy, and two sets of possibilities for success and failure, with all the attendant hopes, anxieties, and fears. Student–athletes really or perceptually encounter bias and prejudice from the student body and especially from faculty members. There are many documented instances of the "jock mentality" among student–athletes, but the vast majority of concerned student–athletes in the 900–odd member institutions in the NCAA and the AIAW are conscientious and capable students.

Undeniably there are abuses and corruptions in inter-collegiate sports and athletics, and the most effective sources and channels for meaningful reform are concerned college presidents and administrators working with efficiently organized national governing bodies for male and female sports. College administrators must reject the "win at any cost syndrome" (in the name of financial prosperity), and bring about a "transvaluation of values" to guarantee meaningful educational opportunity along with successful athletic participation. Sports and athletics are essential and productive in the educational process, especially at the college level, but sports programs must be conducted ethically and morally with the student-athlete's academic well-being as the first priority. Such programs can and should be *winning* programs, but always with priorities properly ordered and with honor, decency, and integrity for the institution and student-athletes.

Closely related to the issue of intercollegiate sports and athletics is the controversy over the importance of *winning* in the sporting enterprise. One of the most frequently quoted and most castigated slogans in this context is the phrase originated by Jim Tatum but more commonly attributed to Vince Lombardi, "Winning isn't everything—it's the only thing." Despite the critical commentary by well-intentioned sports moralists who interpret this to their own advantage, the Tatum-Lombardi contention is fundamentally true—so long as it is properly understood and interpreted. This book defends the thesis that winning *with honor and decency and compassion* is the essence of sports and athletics and life itself. People who say that winning is not important are simply preparing for failure in sports and athletics or whatever the activity might be. People who say that winning is more important than decency and honor and integrity are a disgrace to sports and athletics and a disgrace to the human race.

Common objections to the notion that winning is everything usually reduce to two divergent theories: (1) over-emphasis on winning is incompatible with ethics and morals; and (2) it is more important to compete for its own sake than to compete to win. As already indicated, winning without honor and decency is antithetical to sports and athletics and life itself. No self-respecting person or institution advocates winning at any cost to human integrity or human dignity. Winning is essential, but always within the rules of the game and the rules of authentic human behavior, otherwise the excellence is never true excellence and the victory is a sham. As suggested earlier, the excessive emphasis on winning at any cost in sports and athletics is symptomatic of the same tendency in society at large. What is true of people in general is true of people in sports and athletics, and the remedy is the same for both areas.

Competition for its own sake, without the intent or the desire to win, is at best a hollow victory and is more likely a subterfuge for the acceptance of defeat. This relates to the fundamental nature and purpose of sports and athletics. In their own sophisticated way, the ancient Greeks maintained that "winning is the only thing" and totally rejected second- and third-place finishes and the concept of competing simply for the experience. This attitude prevailed in the Western world until the nineteenth century British ideal expressed in the hallowed adage "it matters not whether you win or lose, but how you play the game."

This sentiment probably has its own rewards, but Western

society is much more aligned to the Grecian ideal of competing to win the prize. For better or worse, we are convinced that it *does* matter whether you win or lose, and not just how you play the game. And significantly this is true even in our most prestigious educational institutions: scholars who simply compete without winning renowned scholastic prizes do not enter such institutions, and they do not teach or become administrators in such institutions. Winning with honor, decency, and integrity is important, but *winning* is the key word. In the final analysis, there is no reason to separate competing with the desire to win from the desire to compete well—they should go hand in hand and usually do. There is a certain nobility in losing as long as maximum effort is expended, but winning is always the positive dimension, and every human endeavor is measured by the Holy Grail of victory.

In a book unparalleled for intense personal conviction and poetic erudition, Michael Novak's *The Joy of Sports* portrays the fulfillment of thought and action in the sporting experience as a joyful and inspirational expression of the human spirit. He contends that sports and athletics constitute the heart of human reality because they best reveal the fundamental virtues of courage, honesty, freedom, community, and excellence. The sporting enterprise is the "chief civilizing agency in our society and culture," and is an authentic and classic form of natural religion.

The spirit of play expressed in sports and athletics defines human existence and human nature much better than the tradition of work and the world of seriousness. Contrary to historical and traditional views, play is the true reality and work is diversion and escape: work is the "kingdom of means," but play is the "kingdom of ends." Work is *necessary* but essentially insignificant as an expression of the human spirit; play is *natural* and makes us what we are and what we strive to be. The vaunted vehicles of progress and civilization, the ostensibly real and serious human pursuits of politics, education, and religion, have not really improved the world over the centuries, but have simply changed some of our perspectives.

Sports and athletics are not the only important concerns in human life, but they are *equally* important and more fundamental compared to commonly accepted and culturally approved contexts for human achievement. The humanizing and civilizing capacity of sports and athletics has been mistakenly ignored and unfairly minimized. People who have no real interest or appreciation for politics, the arts, and education are deficient in the components of true humanity, but the same can be said for people who have no real interest or appreciation for the sporting experience. Sports and athletics are much more than the pastimes of childhood and adolescence—at any age they are serious human pursuits whose depth, intensity, and opportunity for humanistic growth increase in the maturity of adulthood. The values of sports and athletics are the values of life and a lifetime, and befit and enhance the sagacity of age even more than they provide for the joys of youth.

Properly evaluated and interpreted, the world of sports and athletics has a remarkably evident religious character comparable in scope and detail to traditional religious concepts and practices. Traditional religions require faith and belief in the activity itself and in the God or gods who define the religious experience. Sports and athletics also require faith and belief in the possibility of personal salvation through the achievement of human excellence. Traditional religions are value-oriented and concerned with ethics and morality. Sports and athletics are equally value-oriented and are measured by their adherence to ethical and moral principles. Traditional religions have their hierarchies of deities and sacred personnel: concepts of God; saints or persons of consecrated memory; and priests, rabbis, and ministers. Sports and athletics have similar hierarchies: unnamed divinities of the game; legendary sports heroes; and players and coaches who conduct the sporting rituals.

These are but a few indications of the religiosity and

spiritual richness of serious athletic involvement. The depth and credence of social institutions are directly proportionate to the depth and credence of the values and commitments they generate, and this is the common measure of sports and athletics and the religious experience. Like other worlds of special promise and beauty, the world of sports and athletics is secret to the disinterested and the uninitiated. There is a dimension of worthiness to be achieved to understand "the beauties possible" in such a world. "Seven seals lock the inner life of sports (but) they may be broken, one by one." The seven seals reflect the mystic appeal of the sporting experience: *sacred time* and *sacred space; the bond of brothers; rooting* and *agon;* and *competing* and *self-discovery.* To unlock these seals is to experience the joy of sports and athletics.

In every sphere of serious human activity, it is always intriguing to speculate on the nature of things to come. Projections about the future of sports and athletics are fraught with the same difficulties inherent in forecasting the future in other areas of human concern. The principles involved in the future of sports and athletics are the following: (a) the sporting enterprise constitutes a microcosm of society and will continue to reflect social and cultural developments; (b) the spirit of *agon-alea* (competition and chance) is intrinsic in human experience and will prevail unless totally destroyed by life-altering forms of sociopolitical control; and (c) in the apocalyptic event of the destruction of civilization as we know it, the signs of its renaissance will be renewed forms of friendly competition among people and nations.

Speculations about the future of sports and athletics reduce to three basic areas or categories: (1) the *functional* or *structural* area; (2) the "great reformation" area; and (3) the *cosmic* or *futuristic* area. The functional or structural area involves innovative physical developments, such as domed stadiums and diversified indoor facilities, and also organizational innovations, such as national and international expansion of leagues and conferences in most sports. The "great reformation" area relates to ways and means of eliminating abuses and corruptions in the sporting enterprise and is therefore the most pressing issue of contemporary concern about the future viability of sports and athletics.

This is also the most complex area for many reasons, beginning with the fact that abuses and corruptions in sports (and therefore reforms) are related to the economic implications and consequences of the "win at any cost syndrome." This makes predictions and plans for reform multifaceted and complicated, and eventually dependent on socioeconomic attitudes beyond the immediate context of the sporting enterprise. As suggested earlier, sports and athletics reflect trends and themes in our socioeconomic structure and will therefore follow economic indicators wherever these lead for society in general. Our best hope for reform in this area is an educational reorientation of humanistic goals and purposes in an age of secular diversion, and this is perhaps more an ide than a probability.

The cosmic or futuristic area of things to come is poten ly the most complicated and the most awesome because volves the most radical forms of alteration in human a including sports and athletics. We live in an age of s technology with significant consequences for recognition and creative individuality. Our soc structure is characterized by increasing tendenc depersonalization and dehumanization. Too of our self-identity in social security numbers, co outs, and other artifacts of technological effici

Hopefully we will never evolve into an mindless and faceless souls depicted in Georg but the technology exists for a scientifically ty with disastrous consequences for huma sporting experience. The future of sports tertwined with the future of true human tion of humanity as we know it will s end of the sporting enterprise. Sports a mankind's passion for competition and chance and constitute the source and the bastion of cherished human values. True humanism requires the free and creative expression of these passions and values, and this freedom and creativity define the essence of man at play.

In the words of St. Paul, the message of this book is that the world of sports and athletics is a fine and noble place "in which to live and move and have our being." If your heart is hardened to the voices of the athletic ages, if you truly cannot appreciate the unique euphoria of victory and the silent despair of public defeat, if the spirit of the sporting challenge escapes you—well then, my friend, each of us must decide who is the winner and who is the loser.

CHAPTER ONE

Sports and Athletics in Human Existence

The unexamined life is not worth living.

Our uniqueness in the world derives from a strange source: our essential nothingness. We are free and unbounded, and so we can stand back from *things* and question our own existence. Our ability to question is the expression of the spirit.

All work and no play makes Jack a dull boy.

M ankind has diverse needs and desires suited to our existence in the physical world, but our most distinctive need and desire is the challenge of the human spirit. We are unique among denizens of the universe in our ability to transcend physical limitations and *challenge* the world through our intelligence and vision. It is not enough for us simply to exist: we need to question our existence and confront our own destiny and the future of the species. We perceive our imperfections, and we are obsessed with the possibility of perfection in our own lives and in our collective consciousness. We delight in daring ourselves to become better than we are. The challenge of the human spirit occurs in many contexts, but one of the most common and visible is the world of sports and athletics as the supreme analogy of life itself.

As indicated in the introductory chapter, sports and athletics are more than fun and games, and more than idle diversion and mass entertainment for the sports fans of the world. Sports and athletics are philosophical and humanistic in character and contribute significantly to the meaning of mankind and the shaping of civilization. Along with our more esoteric desires for knowledge, love, and aesthetic fulfillment, the sporting experience is inherent in human nature and characterizes the human spirit. In her "Sports and the Cultures of Man," Florence S. Frederickson contends that "there is no society known to man which does not have games of the sort in which individuals set up purely artificial obstacles and get satisfaction from overcoming them."[1] Our own fascination with sports and athletics is reflected in Harry Edwards' contention in *Sociology of Sport* (1973) that "there is literally no institution or stratum in American society which is not touched in some manner by sport."[2]

Some of the great writers and serious minds in the history of mankind have commented on the virtues and values of sports and athletics. The list begins with the ancient epic poet Homer and the classical Greek thinkers Plato and Aristotle, and includes such figures as the Duke of Wellington, General Douglas MacArthur, Arnold Toynbee, Thorstein Veblen, Theodore Dreiser, Presidents Theodore Roosevelt and John F. Kennedy, philosophers George Santayana, Paul Weiss, and Michael Novak, and literary figures such as Ernest Hemingway, Paul Gallico, Damon Runyon, Ring Lardner, Heywood Hale Broun, and James Michener. Some of the sports personalities quoted in this context include Knute Rockne, Vince Lombardi, Red Blaik, Bill Bradley, John Wooden, Joe Paterno, and Morgan Wootten.[3]

Paul Weiss contends that sports and athletics are philosophical and humanistic in character because they provide the greatest opportunity for the greatest number of people to achieve and to witness human excellence. Human excellence in any form naturally excites us and fascinates us, and we strive to achieve excellence or to share vicariously in the achievement of excellence by others. This relates directly to the case for intercollegiate athletics (one of the main areas of emphasis in this book), since the traditional concern of colleges and universities is the pursuit of human excellence in theory and practice. Michael Novak asserts that sports and athletics constitute the most universal social context for human values such as courage, honesty, freedom, community, and excellence, and thus represent the chief civilizing agency in our society and culture. Sports and athletics are based on worthy struggle and competition, and thereby simulate the principles inherent in our concept of civilization.

Contemporary Literature and Historical Sources

The definitive contemporary works specifically in the philosophy and theology of sports and athletics are Paul Weiss' *Sport: A Philosophic Inquiry* (1969), and Michael Novak's *The Joy of Sports* (1976). In a somewhat different vein, Earle Zeigler has written extensively in the field beginning with his *Philosophical Foundations for Physical, Health and Recreation Education* (1964). Robert G. Osterhoudt has edited a valuable collection of original essays in *The Philosophy of Sport* (1973). Howard S. Slusher presents an existentialist philosophy of sports and athletics in *Man, Sport and Existence* (1967), and Harold VanderZwaag describes an essentialist approach in *Toward a Philosophy of Sport* (1972). *The Sporting Spirit* (1977) is an excellent literary version of the philosophy of sports and athletics. James Michener's *Sports in America* (1976) is typical of his extensively researched sociocultural commentaries. More popularized works include Vince Lombardi's *Run to Daylight* (1963), John Wooden's *They Call Me Coach* (1973), John McPhee's *A Sense of Where You Are* (1965), *Joe Paterno: Football My Way* (1978), and Morgan Wootten's *From Orphans to Champions* (1979).[4]

Many of the authors and references cited previously and in later discussions represent a pioneer band of serious scholars associated with the Philosophic Society for the Study of Sport (PSSS). With Paul Weiss as founding president, the PSSS was established in 1972 as an international organization for pedagogy and research in the philosophical and humanistic aspects of sports and athletics. The founding of the PSSS and its dedicated efforts constitute a critical development in scholarly concern and investigation, and the organization serves to correct a historical paradox of neglect for serious philosophical research and publication in sports and athletics. This study contends that sports and athletics are a perennial and universal influence in human existence and experience, and yet relatively little scholarly thought and writing is devoted to the *philosophy* (and theology) of sports and athletics prior to the past three or four decades. This is true historically even from the time of the early Greek philosophers who were notably so prolific and who represented a society of celebrated concern with athletic prowess, and yet they wrote of sports and athletics only briefly and in the context of other issues.

This relative paucity of academic treatises in the philosophy of sports and athletics continues through the ages to the beginning of the current century, when more frequent but still sporadic publications become available in this country and to an increasing extent in other countries. Typical bibliographical examples of this emerging interest include George Santayana's "Philosophy on the Bleachers" (1894), H. Graves' "A Philosophy of Sport" (1917), Elmer Berry's "The Philosophy of Athletics" (1927), John Krout's *Annals of American Sport* (1929), and Peter McBride's *The Philosophy of Sport* (1933). An excellent summary and commentary on the historical development of serious works on the philosophy of sports and athletics is included in *Sport and Society: An Anthology* (1973).[5]

The PSSS has provided invaluable service in coordinating and cataloging historical and contemporary research and pedagogical techniques, and most importantly in encouraging continued and increased academic concern in the field. The Society's most recent bibliography lists approximately 650 items reflecting critical historical interest and immensely varied philosophical insight. In addition to the authors already cited, some of the more prolific writers represented include Carolyn E. Thomas, William J. Morgan, Klaus V. Meier, Warren P. Fraleigh, R. Scott Kretchmar, Hans Lenk, Paul Kuntz, Seymour Kleinman, and James W. Keating. The PSSS publishes *The Journal of the Philosophy of Sport* "to foster philosophic interchange among scholars interested in better understanding sport."[6]

Sins of the Flesh in Sports and Athletics

What was said earlier about the historical significance and philosophical values and virtues of sports and athletics is high praise indeed, and this engenders some tempering commentary on the failures of the flesh in the sporting enterprise. As already suggested, sports and atlethics are similar to other important areas of human activity in having within themselves the potentiality and the reality of corruption and abuse. Critics and detractors of sports and athletics have also existed from ancient times to our own days, and have sometimes justifiably scored the deficiencies in spirit and motivation and purposes in sports and athletics.[7] Such criticism is understandable and serves to balance an honest and objective appraisal. Philosophical and humanistic views of sports and athletics must relate such activites to the ethical and moral principles that govern all human conduct and human striving. Sports and athletics must abide by the rules of life and the rules of the game, since otherwise the excellence is never true excellence and the victory is a sham. Peter McIntosh's scholarly and thorough *Fair Play* (1979) discusses ethics in sports and education and concludes that "moral decisions in sport are inescapable. If sport in any of its manifold forms is included in the education of children—and it is difficult to envisage its total exclusion—then moral decisions must be made. If they are not made consciously and deliberately, moral standpoints will still be adopted but unconsciously and irrationally."[8]

Especially in contemporary society with the emergence of commercialism and professionalism in so many aspects of the sporting enterprise, it is true that sports and athletics have sometimes been subverted and corrupted by socioeconomic interests with an attendant immorality totally contrary to the nature and purpose of the game. Examples are all too evident and begin perhaps with the tainting of the sacred ideals of the original Olympiads in the name of political and national recognition, and the resultant professionalizing of the Games through private and corporate subsidies for athletes and entire programs. There is strong evidence that some individuals and some organizations in contemporary sports have grossly misinterpreted the nature and importance of winning, and read this to mean that victory should be pursued at any and every cost to human decency and integrity. This "win at any cost" syndrome is reflected in the excessively competitive character of contemporary sports and athletics, and the tendency of unscrupulous administrators and coaches to resort to dehumanizing tactics to ensure victory.

One of the derivative areas of common criticism leveled at sports and athletics cites an over-emphasis on violence and aggression for its own sake, and a catering to the pernicious sadistic element lurking in society. Robert C. Yeager analyzes this aspect of sports and athletics in his incisive *Seasons of Shame: The New Violence in Sports* (1979).[9] Another much-publicized condemnation of the sporting enterprise involves allegations of wide-spread illicit and medically questionable drug usage among athletes, provoking understandable suspicion in the public mind about the probity and humaneness of sports motivation. Other dubious ethical and moral practices include the absurdly excessive salaries paid to professional players and coaches; the contract-jumping by professional players and coaches for economic reasons (reflected in similar moves by college coaches for the same reasons and transfers by college athletes from one institution to another); and even the spectacle of famous sports heroes literally cashing in on athletic fame by huckstering products in television commercials.

Probably the most grievous fault in contemporary sports and athletics is the exploitation of intercollegiate athletes for athletic purposes with little or no regard for their academic progress and graduation. Commonly cited irregularities begin with illegal and immoral recruiting inducements to attend given institutions, and then the mandating of academically flimsy programs of study specially designed for student-athletes (sometimes involving mythical courses and fabricated transcripts). The usual tragic result is the de facto denial of the educational process in the name of guaranteeing athletic eligibility and productivity. It must be observed that the vast majority of colleges and universities conduct ethically sound sports programs (and the vast majority of intercollegiate athletes are sincere students), but the odious character of even a few such transgressions has invited extensive criticism from a variety of concerned sources.[10]

Sports as a Microcosm of Society

One explanation or rationale for all these deficiencies is that sports and athletics constitute a microcosm of society and thus tend to reflect the ills of an essentially commercial and overly competitive social structure. Penn State University athletic director and football coach Joe Paterno, noted for his philosophical and humanistic approach to sports and athletics, says categorically that "excesses in sports are a microcosm of society. When society stops cheating, then we can expect the same of intercollegiate sports." Ours is a society with tendencies toward violence and aggression expressed in mounting crime statistics and terroristic acts and the proclivity of groups and nations to resort to military force. Ours is a society of intense competition where success is imperative (sometimes at dubious cost) and where supremacy is usually measured by secular and mercenary standards. In politics and industry and other significant areas, this has led to the betrayal of trusts and the destruction of careers and the breaking of dreams and lives. The disturbing messages of Watergate and Abscam and *Patterns* and *Executive Suite* suggest that the spirit of our land is frequently embodied in pragmatic expediency.

Professional athletes expect a monetary return for their highly acclaimed public services comparable to the millions of dollars in salaries and fees paid to rock groups, hosts of television talk shows, news commentators, and other public figures and private business executives. Extensive and illicit drug use and abuse is a much-discussed social, moral, and legal problem involving the highest levels of government as well as public entertainers, young professionals, and every stratum of society. Dreams and sins of greed and avarice are by no means limited to the world of sports and athletics. One of the most poetic critiques of the sporting enterprise is recited in Michael Novak's *The Joy of Sports*:

> There are priests who mumble through the Mass, lovers who read letters over a naked shoulder in love's embrace, teachers who detest students, pedants who shrink from original ideas. So also there are athletes and fans and sportswriters who never grasp the beauty or the treasure entrusted to them. It must not be imagined that the mysteries of sport are directly penetrated. Much depends on the qualities of heart of the pursuer. A hundred young men tugged at Excalibur; only Arthur could pull it from the rock. There are, in suitable proportion, vulgar and sotted and distasteful men in sports. There are minimal perceptions, manipulations, deals and compromises. There are hucksters and profiteers and egomaniacs. It is not required by sports, whether in fan or athlete or journalist, that one be virtuous; if that were so, many millions could not love the game. But the failures of human flesh to measure up to the beauties possible in sports should not deter us from pursuing what is in them that draws so on our love.[11]

More extensive and more vehement denunciations of sports and athletics in contemporary literature include Leonard Shecter's *The Jocks* (1969), Dave Meggyesy's *Out of Their League* (1971), Jack Scott's *The Athletic Revolution* (1971), Paul Hoch's *Rip Off the Big Game* (1972), and Peter Gent's *North Dallas Forty* (1973).[12] The pragmatic reduction in all this is that if millions of people are willing to pay millions of dollars to support our present athletic structures and policies, then probably this is what we all deserve. When society revises its ideals and value-standards, then the world of sports and athletics will more clearly reflect "the beauties possible" and will become more fitting for our love.

Work and Play: Concepts and Definitions

In a theoretical or chronological sense, this survey begins with the basic concepts of work and leisure time and then the derivative concepts of play and games (and sports and athletics) as distinctly human pursuits. Scholarly definitions of play and games (and eventually sports and athletics) involve fundamental distinctions between these activities and "the world of work and seriousness." The current classic in this area is Bernard Suits' *The Grasshopper: Games, Life and Utopia* (1978), and earlier standard works are Johan Huizinga's *Homo Ludens* (1950), and Roger Caillois' *Man, Play and Games* (1961). Significant literature in the field has expanded rapidly and among recent valuable works are *Sport and the Body: A Philosophical Symposium* (1972), and *The Philosophical Process in Physical Education* (1977). The most comprehensive survey in the area is *Research in the History, Philosophy and International Aspects of Physical Education and Sport: Bibliographies and Techniques* (1971).[13]

This study settles for relatively simplistic definitions of play and games (and sports and athletics) derived from these diversified sources, and again the fundamental contrast is between "the world of work and seriousness" and the world of play and games. We define work as "essentially nonvoluntary human activity pursued in more or less rigidly prescribed socioeconomic contexts in ordinary space and time and involving definite and usually measurable socioeconomic productivity." Play and games are defined as "freely organized and voluntary human activity with its own spatial and temporal boundaries and having its own purposes and rules apart from routine existence and apart from definite and measurable socioeconomic productivity." Sports constitute an extension of play and games characterized by "recognizable physical exertion and demonstrated skill and a sense of seriousness," and athletics constitute "organized multisport programs at the amateur and intercollegiate and professional levels." This provides an opportunity to explain the sometimes cumbersome and probably ad nauseam use of the phrase "sports and athletics" throughout these pages. As indicated in the preceding definitions, there *is* a distinction between sports and athletics and the intention is to include both areas in all such contexts. References simply to sports seem to be truncated and abrupt, and fall short of the complete view. In some languages and some philosophical circles (notably French), references simply to the *philosophy of sports* can be inaccurate and misleading.[14]

These simplified definitions of play and games and sports and athletics create nuances and subtleties subject to value judgments and individual interpretations. The basic elements of "recognizable physical exertion and demonstrated skill and a sense of seriousness" which distinguish sports and athletics from play and games are flexible and apply in diverse ways. Chess and checkers are normally forms of play and games rather than sports and athletics, but participants in international competition expend considerable physical and mental energy and are quite skillful and undoubtedly serious about the activity. Such presumably sporting activities as bird-watching and dog-training seem to go beyond the category of play and games, and yet seem to fall short in normal circumstances of the puristic concept of sports and athletics.

Especially in contemporary sports and athletics, the most troublesome distinction is the concept of "measurable socioeconomic productivity" relating to our sports world. This is fundamentally a characteristic of the work-world rather than sports and athletics, but is reflected extensively in many areas of the sporting enterprise. Advanced amateur sports (including the Olympics) and intercollegiate sports programs have become business ventures including definite socioeconomic dimensions for the athletes and for the organizations and institutions. Much has been alleged about direct and indirect financing of AAU and Olympic athletes and teams, and all such participation routinely involves significant financial expenditure. Major intercollegiate sports programs operate with multimillion dollar athletic budgets, and the institutional revenue from successful programs runs in some instances literally to millions of dollars. Intercollegiate student-athletes generally receive forms of payment known as athletic grants-in-aid designed to cover tuition and living expenses and related fees, and such grants amount in some cases to tens of thousands of dollars over the four-year period. The primary purpose of athletic grants is to provide educational opportunity for student-athletes, but the roar of the crowd on Saturday afternoons has an economic echo suited to the marketplace as well as the campus.

This socioeconomic dimension in sports and athletics is most evident of course in the immense growth and popularity of professional sports in this country and throughout the world. Professional athletes obviously perform services in return for specified and contractural monetary salaries —some of them enormous on an annual basis and over a period of time. Professional sports franchises reflect investments of vast sums of money in the acquisition and development of the franchise itself, and in the construction of lavish and expensive stadiums which become architectural marvels and cultural showcases. Despite periodic controversy and implied denials, these large financial investments presumably bring about suitable financial returns for owners and stockholders. For many wealthy sports buffs, the dream investment of a lifetime is a major league sports franchise in whatever sport is available. This is reflected in perhaps the most evident business aspect of contemporary sports and athletics: many sports franchises are now subsidiaries of corporate enterprises in such diversified areas as restaurant chains, transportation, drugs and health improvement industries, and even book-publishing. This has caused serious and justifiable concern within and without the sporting enterprise about the effect of this potentially disinterested business control on the integrity and purity of the game. The loyalty is not so much to the team or to sports and athletics, but to the prospects for solvency and financial success.[15]

Any lingering doubts about the business orientation of contemporary sports and athletics should be dispelled by the major league baseball players strike in 1981 (and threatened strikes by professional players in other sports). There is no real merit in assigning blame for the strike primarily to the owners or primarily to the players—obviously both were involved, and the only real tragedy is that it happened. The owners and the players pricked the magic balloon and destroyed the ideal that professional athletes are *somehow* different from bus-drivers, nurses, schoolteachers, steelmill workers, miners, construction workers, and postal employees who strike or threaten to strike as a means of employment control. If professional athletes insist on viewing themselves (when it is convenient) simply as another segment of the working force, then perhaps we should restructure the sporting enterprise to reflect working conditions consistent with other forms of unionized occupations: five-day work weeks, hourly wages or compensation, regulated sick time and vacation time, company sponsored health and dental plans, and retirement at age 65 or earlier with reduced benefits. The beautiful aspiration of *playing* for a living has succumbed to the need for money and security, and the game will never be the same. And the final irony is that never before (and possibly never again) will the money and the security in most professional sports be as ample as it is today.

The baseball players strike undoubtedly contributed to the ominous possibility of government intervention and control in sports and athletics, expressed in Congressional and Senate committee hearings and Justice Department evaluations of the structure and purpose of sports and athletics. The preliminary consensus (not surprisingly) is that professional sports are business and should be subject to antitrust laws and other federal legislation applicable to other unregulated sectors of the economy. Probably the moral here is that what one sows, one will reap. If some participants in the sporting enterprise insist on living by the precepts of the work-world when it suits their convenience, then they must accept the consequences of their abdication from the protected realm of heroes and artists. It is one of the compelling mysteries of sports and athletics that people should be involved for the love of the game rather than for economic profit. In a final resolution of the question as to whether serious athletes play for a living or work for a living (they do both), it might be maintained that serious athletes "enjoy their work" more than members of other professions, and this element of joy and self-satisfaction will forever distinguish the world of sports and athletics from the world of work and seriousness.

Programs of Sports Studies

Along with the philosophy of sports and athletics, courses in the psychology and sociology of sports (and other approaches) are emerging rapidly and have become popular curriculum listings in numerous colleges and universities across the nation. A survey by the University of California in 1978 indicates that at least twenty universities offer graduate programs in sports studies, primarily in the areas of sports administration and sports management.[16] The logical institutional extension of this is to introduce entire programs of sports studies centering perhaps on the philosophy of sports and athletics but also extending into various areas in the field. Some efforts have been initiated in this direction, exemplified in the University of Massachusetts' Department of Sports Studies and Sports Management, and the University of Waterloo's (Ontario) Faculty of Human Kinetics and Leisure Studies.

In the interests of fostering further thought on the issue, this chapter concludes with a modest proposal for the basic content of a program of sports studies for the undergraduate curriculum. These are suggested descriptions for the various courses and suggested combinations of areas, but the content and structure of the program are flexible and subject to personal preferences. Any planning to institute such a program requires careful evaluation of the current and future availability of qualified teaching personnel within the institution, although the use of audiovisual materials and guest experts will alleviate the burdens of preparation and presentation. Whether such programs should lead to specific academic degrees is an issue that individual institutions must decide according to their internal purposes and goals.

Suggested Program in Sports Studies

I.   *Work and Culture*

A preliminary investigation of the nature of work and the relationship between work and other dimensions of human life, especially the concepts of leisure time and play.

II.   *Philosophy of Sports and Athletics*

An inquiry into the philosophical and humanistic aspects of sports and athletics and their significance as a basic human experience; sports and athletics as a means of achieving human excellence and as the basis of society and culture.

III.   *Psychology and Sociology of Sports and Athletics*

a) An inquiry into theories of motivation achievement in sports and in human existence; theories on success and failure attitudes; theories on psychological typing and stereotyping in sports and athletics and in human existence.

b) A survey of the historic and present social culture of sports and athletics viewed as a social institution; social role of play and games and sports and athletics in society and culture.

IV.   *Sports Administration and Sports Management*

An evaluation of the special problems in the business administration of multimillion dollar sports enterprises; legal and moral implications of sports and athletics as big business in the national economy.

a) Sports Law: An evaluation of special problems in legal aspects of sports and athletics in general and in sports unions and players associations; sports contracts and legal and moral due process in liability considerations.

V. *Sports and Athletics as Philosophical Literature*

A survey and analysis of philosophical principles in the dramatic and anecdotal past and present of sports in the folklore and literature of the world.

a) Sports and the Media: An inquiry into the enterprise of sports publicity and sports reporting in its nature, content, and purpose.

VI. *Sports Medicine*

A survey and evaluation of the rapidly growing area of specialized medical concern in prevention and treatment of sports injuries and the science of physical fitness in general; consideration of the ethical and moral aspects of sports medicine in general and in preparation for athletic participation.

VII. *Sports and Statistics*

An inquiry into the mathematical context and basis for sports achievement, and the statistical foundation for the business of betting and handicapping.

CHAPTER TWO

The Pursuit
of
Excellence

P receding discussions asserted that sports and athletics are demonstrably ubiquitous throughout human history in the most diverse societies and cultures and contribute significantly to the meaning of mankind. Following Paul Weiss' definitive views and critical insights in *Sport: A Philosophic Inquiry*, this chapter provides an explication and rationale for mankind's timeless and universal fascination with sports and athletics in the context of human achievement.[1] Part of the historical paradox of neglect with respect to sports and athletics is that cultural commentators have long extolled scholar-intellectuals for their contributions to the progress and well-being of humanity, but relatively little has been said about the contributions of athletes in the development of civilization and the definition of the human spirit. Perhaps more than any other form of human activity, sports and athletics more frequently and more dramatically plumb the heights and depths of human experience and truly realize the ecstasy and the agony of human striving. "An athlete once was, and still can be, treated as a sacred being who embodies something of the divine in him. He is credited with the dignity of embodying a supreme value."[2]

This chapter analyzes the philosophical and humanistic dimensions of sports and athletics, and proposes the most comprehensive explanation for mankind's perennial interest and indulgence in the sporting experience. Many partial explanations are frequently suggested, but the total explanation must include the realistic intentions and desires of *participants* and must relate also to *spectators* who constitute such an intrinsic aspect of sports and athletics. Probably the most popular partial answers reduce to four areas of interest and concern, all of which convey part of the rationale but singly and together fall short of the complete explanation either in scope or applicability. These answers are the following: a) sports and athletics build character and develop sound and virtous human qualities; b) sports and athletics develop a social sense or a sense of human community; c) sports and athletics constitute an opportunity for "upward mobility" through fame and fortune; and d) sports and athletics constitute an acceptable and permissible outlet for violence and aggression in participants and in spectators.[3]

Sports and Character Development

The contention that sports and athletics build character and develop sound human qualities is true to some extent, but has certain deficiencies and limitations with respect to the complete explanation of the popularity of sports and athletics. A common contention in psychological studies is that one's character is largely formed early in life (probably in the period from one to five years of age), and thus is formed considerably before potential athletes become seriously interested in sports and athletics even at the little league stages. The classic research in this area is attributed to Dr. Bruce Ogilvie and Dr. Thomas A. Tutko, whose psychiatric and psychological studies on this point are summarized in their often-quoted article "Sport: If You Want to Build Character Try Something Else" (October 1971). Their extensive and professional scientific research led them to the significant though simply stated conclusion: "We found no empirical evidence that sport builds character."[4]

It seems true enough that sports and athletics *reveal* character, and clearly indicate (sometimes for the world to see) whether an athlete possesses the qualities of courage, self-reliance, and ability achieved through hard work and self-sacrifice. There are so many pressure situations in sports and athletics relating to this (the basketball player on the foul line in a tie game with no time left and an opportunity to win the game—usually to the accompaniment of distracting crowd reaction), and it is apparent that such situations reveal the athlete's character and ability to control mind, emotions, and body in truly challenging circumstances. There is another difficulty in the "sports build character" answer to the reason for the universal popularity of sports and athletics, and this is the difficulty in applying or relating this notion in any realistic way to the spectators involved. There seems to be little if any overt opportunity for character-building among spectators at sporting events, and so this remains at best an approximate answer to the issue at hand.

Social Community: Players and Spectators

The second partial explanation for the universal appeal of sports and athletics is the contention that such activities develop our social sense or a sense of human community. Again this is true to some extent in some sports and perhaps generally in the sporting experience, but the fact is that many popular sports are individual forms of competition (with one's self and/or nature) with little or no opportunity or real desire for social community. Examples of such sports would be golf, diving, skiing, many track and field events, and horse racing. Probably such activities initiate and foster a sense of comraderie among participants struggling with the same types of obstacles and difficulties, but the emphasis consistently is on individual participation and individual triumph or defeat. Despite all the hallowed emphasis even in team sports on the importance of team spirit and team cooperation, there is reason to contend that individual team members tend to be acutely conscious of themselves and their own efforts and judgment about success and failure.

This concept of social community in sports and athletics applies positively and in a curiously negative way to sports fans and spectators. Undoubtedly spectators at sporting events experience a strong sense of communal bonding in the context of their mutual presence and interest in the event, and the larger the crowd and the more significant the event, the more intense the experience becomes. In his *The Joy of Sports*, Michael Novak talks eloquently about the joys and the importance of *rooting* for favored sports teams.

> To be a fan is totally in keeping with being a man. To have particular loyalties is not to be deficient in universality, but to be faithful to the laws of human finitude. A team is not only *assembled* in one place; it also represents a place. Location is not merely a bodily necessity; it gives rise to a new psychological reality . . . . In sports cities around the nation, millions of lives are affected by whether in the days of their youth they were privileged to cheer for winners or, good-naturedly, groaningly, grew up with perennial losers . . . To watch a sports event is not like watching a set of abstract patterns. It is to take a risk, to root and to be rooted . . . . The mode of observation proper to a sports event is *to participate*—that is to extend one's own identification to one side, and to absorb with it the blows of fortune, to join with that team in testing the favors of the Fates.[5]

In his *Man, Play and Games*, Roger Caillois discusses sports fans in the context of *mimicry* as one of four basic game categories (these game categories and their principles are described and analyzed in the following chapter). Mimicry is a game form involving structured and unstructured attempts to imitate or simulate both other people and some rituals and symbols of nature in general. Caillois points out that sports fans share vicariously in the game or the sports event, and imitate the participants even with bodily movements suited to the movements of the players in the game. This mimicry-adulation extends in some cases (especially in younger fans) to mental identity with the players, and it is fairly common nowadays to see some sports fans emulate favored athletes even in physical appearance, dress codes, and mannerisms.

These comments about the positive aspects of social community in sports fans contrast with a fundamental dimension of existentialist philosophy applied to sports and athletics (existentialist philosophy in sports and athletics is discussed extensively in chapter IV). Existentialist philosophy is founded on the primacy and dignity of the human reality as an individual, and emphasizes the importance of self-identity and self-consciousness and the essential need to avoid all forms of self-alienation and self-estrangement. This suggests a critical issue in the application of the social community theme to sports and athletics especially with respect to sports spectators. In the existentialist view of life and human activities, all attempts at serious mimicry or identification with others (including sports participants) are anathema and contradictory to the personal identity and integrity that constitute authentic human existence. One possible solution or resolution within the context of existentialist philosophy itself is reflected in the existentialist views of Gabriel Marcel (1889-1973), a French Catholic existentialist and probably the most respected exponent of Christian existentialism. Marcel's existentialism is unique in that he emphasizes intersubjectivity and intercommunity along with personal subjectivity and personal authenticity. Marcel's creed is *esse est coesse*—"to be (to exist) is to be with others" and with God.[6] Such an approach could constitute the basis for an existentialist application of the social community theory in sports and athletics relating to sports spectators.

Upward Mobility and the Impossible Dream

The third commonly offered partial explanation for the timeless and universal popularity of sports and athletics is particularly prevalent in contemporary society, and this is the "upward mobility" theory or the notion that sports and athletics constitute a lure and an opportunity for fame and material prosperity. This view is propounded in various overt and subtle ways to the youth of the world, and is especially applicable to minority athletes in America and in other nations as well. The dubious validity of this contention has been investigated and exposed by numerous commentators on the amateur and intercollegiate and professional levels of sports and athletics. James A. Michener's *Sports in America* includes an unusually comprehensive and thoroughly documented analysis of "Sports and Upward Escalation" centering mainly on black athletes with references to other minority groups.[7] Television's *60 Minutes* (February 1980) depicted a shocking revelation of the exploitation of college athletes obsessed with the dream of "making it big in the pros."[8] Pertinent scholarly references to the issue are included in M. Marie Hart's *Sports in the Socio-Cultural Process.*[9]

Deficiencies in this partial explanation for the popularity of sports and athletics are obvious and begin with the fact that the vast majority of people who participate in sports and athletics do so without any hope or even desire to achieve fame and material prosperity. This would apply to the millions of amateur sports participants as individuals and as members of sports organizations throughout the world. Among those who do aspire (realistically or unrealistically) to be professional athletes, empirical studies indicate that a miniscule proportion (the usual figure is two percent) ever achieve this goal, and an even smaller percentage receive the huge and highly publicized contracts which have become the symbol of financial success through sports and athletics. Since the advent of free agency clauses in professional baseball contracts within the past five years (and variations of this in other sports), average salaries in the popular sports have become ridiculously high—in the hundreds of thousands of dollars per year and in the millions of dollars over a period of time. Apart from this innovation, and apart from the inflationary spiral afflicting wages and prices throughout our national economy, it might still be maintained that average salaries for *all* professional athletes in *all* sports are roughly comparable to personal income in many less glamorized fields of endeavor. The current minimum salary for major league baseball players is around $35,000 (and much less in some other sports), and this compares with starting salaries for M.B.A. graduates from prestigious institutions.[10]

Sports as an Outlet for Violence and Aggression

The fourth and final partial explanation for the universal fascination with sports and athletics is historically and popularly proposed, and this is the notion that sports and athletics constitute an accepted and permissible outlet for violence and aggression. This has been suggested or implied since the days of the ancient gladiators and other forms of sadistic sport, and certainly in today's sporting world there is justifiable concern about violence and aggression and their positive and negative influence on participants and spectators. Numerous studies in contemporary sports literature decry the principle of violence and aggression in sports and athletics and its increasing application as an integral dimension in the sporting experience. In his comprehensive and well-researched *Seasons of Shame*, Robert C. Yeager asserts that the training of athletes has never before seemed so deliberately violent and so widespread throughout the sporting enterprise.[11]

It is unfortunately true that violence and aggression have always exerted a curious attraction for mankind, but it has yet to be proved that mankind is essentially violent and aggressive by nature. The sadistic element lurks in human nature and some historical heroes (or antiheroes) have been violent and aggressive people, but some of the most revered figures in human history have been pacifists and martyrs and others of similar attitudes for whom violence and aggression are the antithesis of meaningful human existence. Probably some people have extolled Attila the Hun, but many more have admired St. Francis of Assissi and Mahatma Gandhi and Martin Luther King. Few people are attracted to sports and athletics *simply* because of violence and aggression wherever and whenever these exist, and it is also true that many popular sports with historical appeal are nonviolent in nature and still attract considerable followings (golf, tennis, and baseball).

Professional football and professional ice hockey are probably the two most violent sports in America today, and yet it might be speculated that few people would find these sports interesting and attractive if they were somehow compelled to watch *only* the most violent aspects of the game—the line-play in football and the body-checking and stick-play in hockey. Serious participants in such sports can be psychologically exhilarated by the prospect and reality of violence and aggression, and to some extent (in the proper circumstances) this is natural enough and even laudable in the context of our concern with meritorious *agon* or worthy struggle and competition. In his incisive analysis of Paul Weiss' theories on sport, Paul Kuntz describes how violence can be raised even to an art-form by citing the sport of bull-fighting perceived as the "game of games" since the risks are so high and the stakes are life or death.[12] One of the intriguing manifestations of violence in sports involves playing on home fields and home courts as opposed to playing "on the road." Some interesting psychological studies have been conducted relating to players' attitudes when playing before relatives and friends contrasted with playing before hostile strangers. The "home turf" is a significant factor in serious athletic competition, and it has been contended that extensive travelling by professional athletes leads to a sense of frustration and estrangement from families and loved ones, and this is frequently relieved through violent behavior against the opposing (home) team.

Sports and Aesthetics: The Artistry of Execution

Participants and spectators are attracted even to violent sports and athletics not for the violence but for the spectacle of the *total game*. In the final analysis "the game is always the thing," and in the context of the *total game* (and ironically in the context of violence and aggression in sports and athletics), participants and spectators perceive the *artistry of execution* and the significant aesthetic quality of sports and athletics. There is remarkable grace and beauty of physical movement in sports and athletics including elements of the dance in general and forms of the ballet in particular. This is true in most if not all sports in both individual and team activities, and it is curious and rewarding to discover in the sometimes violent world of athletics such ample evidence of bodily rhythm and physical grace. These aesthetic characteristics of sports and athletics relate easily to the essentials and the larger dimensions of the artistic experience and creative productivity. This is portrayed in the following acronym illustrating the ideal qualities of successful aesthetic achievement: *T*ranscendence; *R*evelation; *E*xpressiveness; *A*nalogy; *S*ynthesis; *U*nity; *R*arity; *E*conomy.[13]

Transcendence refers to human experiences whereby we move above and beyond routine or traditional ways of perceiving the world; in transcendence we discern newer and higher values and the experience is larger than life. Sports and athletics transcend ordinary space and time and provide rare and puristic pleasures and insights suited to the view from the mountaintop.

Revelation is openness to oneself and to others—it is self-discovery and personal confrontation. Sports and athletics force us to see ourselves without the facade and the pretense of ordinary experience. We are on the line by ourselves to triumph or to twist slowly in the wind.

Expressiveness reflects the embodiment of the transcendental character of sports and athletics in participants and spectators. In physical actions and personal commitment, participants and spectators reveal the essential meaning of sports and athletics in concrete forms rather than elusive abstractions.

Analogy signifies a common denominator between diverse realities and experiences. Sports and athletics are somewhat similar to ordinary life but also different from ordinary life; they symbolize life and death . . . they start from where we are and show us what we can be.

Synthesis refers to the combination of principles and ideas and actions inherent in successful and meaningful human activities.

The artist and the athlete weave these components into an integrated and beautiful product or experience.

Unity relates to synthesis in that we recognize and experience the oneness and the integrity and the intrinsic truth of artistic creativity and athletic performance.

Rarity indicates that significant works of art and significant athletic achievements are unique and reflect special forms of excellence. This explains their celebrated acceptance and lasting value as masterpieces and the stuff of legends.

Economy emphasizes that excess is the ruination of artistry in any form: creative excellence and athletic excellence reflect a minimum of overt effort and maximum productivity. Artistic creativity and athletic success derive from intense preparation and ability honed to the point of efficient action. This is the substance of the accolade about great athletes: "They make it look so easy."

Much has been written on the aesthetic aspects of sports and athletics, perhaps most notably Eleanor Methany's *Movement and Meaning* (1968), Eugene Kaelin's "The Well-Played Game: Notes Toward an Aesthetics of Sports" (1968), and Hilde Hein's "Performance as an Aesthetic Category" (1970). Gerber and Morgan include a scholarly series of articles on "Sport and Aesthetics" in *Sport and the Body: A Philosophic Symposium*, and a similar collection on "The Aesthetic Status of Sport" appears in Robert Osterhoudt's *The Philosophy of Sport*. Ruth Casper, O. P., proposes a closely reasoned philosophico-aesthetic theory in her "Play Springs Eternal" (1978).[14]

Sports and the Pursuit of Excellence

Enough has been said about these four partial explanations for the timeless and universal appeal of sports and athletics, and their philosophical and humanistic character in human existence and experience. Following Weiss' insights on the issue, the fundamental and comprehensive explanation is that sports and athletics *provide the greatest opportunity for the greatest number of people to achieve and to witness human excellence.*

> Excellence excites and awes. It pleases and it challenges. We are often delighted by splendid specimens whether they be flowers, beasts or men. A superb performance interests us even more because it reveals to us the magnitude of what then can be done. Illustrating perfection, it gives us a measure for whatever else we do.
>
> Unlike other beings we men have the ability to appreciate excellence. We desire to achieve it. We want to share in it. Even though it may point up the fact that we are defective, less than we might have been, we like to look upon it. It is what ought to be.[15]

The excellence involved in sports and athletics is admittedly physical or bodily excellence, but this is true human excellence and contributes to the fulfillment of human existence. We are obviously physical or bodily beings (despite some philosophical disclaimers of the past and present), and it is only natural that we should seek excellence at this level as well as other levels of existence and experience.[16] This form of human excellence is attractive and appealing to sports participants who attempt to achieve this excellence, and it is equally attractive and appealing to spectators who share vicariously in the experience of realizing what man can do and what man can become when pushed to the limits of physical being. There are other forms of human excellence that are significantly appealing to mankind: intellectual and scholarly excellence and spiritual excellence in various forms. The problem is that such forms of excellence are beyond the grasp of the majority, and normally beyond the grasp of the young in particular. Sports and athletics provide a more feasible opportunity for far more people to achieve actually or vicariously an awareness of satisfaction and recognition as fulfilled human realities.

In an interesting interpretation and extension of Weiss'

basic theory, Keith Algozin (1976) discusses the issue in the context of *unalienated action* relating to human purposes and goals.[17] Unalienated action represents those ideal situations wherein we clearly and distinctly perceive the ultimate good and the ultimate evil, where we clearly understand the meaning of victory and the meaning of defeat, and where we clearly know the actions that must be performed to bring about the desired result. Human existence and human experience are fundamentally ambiguous in that too often and to a significant degree we do not clearly perceive and understand what is truly valuable and desirable, and what specific actions we should perform to achieve our goals. There are shadings and doubts and too many moments and forms of indecision about the human condition in its nature and purpose.

The world of sports and athletics is a clear and decisive world of unalienated action where the ultimate value of victory and the ultimate evil of defeat are clearly apparent, and where the purposes and choices and even the tools to use are evident to all who understand the game.

> To enter the world of the game is to leave behind that dimension of ourselves which can doubt and belittle all values, and is to live within a closed system of action whose every present moment is both fully illuminated by a well-defined supreme value and transparently related to every other moment in the whole. . . .
>
> At every moment of the game the athlete is at the center of this translucent system, acting spontaneously from within his immediate apprehension of what everything in his world truly is and requires in light of the whole. At his disposal are the supreme value he is to realize, the unambiguous facts of his situation, and his practiced capacity to counter obvious resistances with obvious tools. He is the picture of action flowing from final judgments and decisions of conscience in appropriate response to the changing situation.[18]

These fundamental philosophical and humanistic dimensions of sports and athletics are elaborated in a series of books and articles by Dr. George Sheehan, an internationally recognized medical authority on sports and physical fitness.

> Most of us should be educated in the good life and how to attain it. In this the athlete provides a much better model than the scholar. . . In his highly visible pursuit of a highly visible perfection, he illustrates the age-old advice to become the person you are. Simply by being himself, the athlete makes a statement that has profound philosophical, psychological, physiological and spiritual implications. . .

> Play is the answer to the puzzle of our existence, the stage for our excesses and exuberances. Play is where life lives, where the game is the game. Some of the good things that play provides are physical grace, psychological ease and personal integrity. Some of the best are the peak experiences, when you have a sense of oneness with yourself and nature. These are truly times of peace the world cannot give. It may be that the hereafter will have them in constant supply; but in the here and now, play is the place to find them, the place where we are constantly being and becoming ourselves.[19]

In mankind's historical and continuing quest for human excellence, there is reason to contend that sports and athletics and the athletes of time and the world best portray the authentic meaning of human striving.

The Case for Intercollegiate Athletics

The contentions and arguments in this chapter relate to the philosophical and humanistic aspects of intercollegiate sports and athletics (an area of central concern discussed extensively in chapters V and VI). Intercollegiate sports and athletics are immensely popular in our society and culture, and constitute an area of convergence and a proving ground for the virtues and values (and abuses and corruptions) in the sporting enterprise. In view of the remarks and viewpoints in this chapter, it is relatively easy to make the case for the importance and the validity of ethically oriented and successful intercollegiate sports and athletic programs as an integral component of contemporary higher education. The argument is that ethically sound and successful sports programs constitute a natural means for achieving human excellence, and the production of human excellence is the reason for being of colleges and universities. The need and the opportunity for physical excellence are apparent in the nature and goals of human existence, and this by no means denies the importance of intellectual and scholarly excellence as the main product of the college experience. The achivement of human excellence in any form is an essential purpose of higher education. Intercollegiate sports and athletic programs should have comparable status and viability consistent with other programs in the institution. Attempts to deal with sports and athletics as expendable afterthoughts or evil necessities undermine the purposes and goals of the educational process.

Intercollegiate sports and athletics have become expansive and expensive empires with the potentiality and reality for abuse and corruption, and some critics contend that a return to more modest intramural sports and athletic programs would be a return to sanity and perspective. This may be true to some extent but it would result in a diluted achievement of human excellence. An essential aspect of sports and athletics is the competitive aspect, and the better the competition the nobler the achievement. If there is value in sports and athletics, then there is the highest value in the most competitive programs and purposes. The measure of true superiority (and therefore the measure of true excellence) comes from competing and winning against the dedicated rivalry represented in diverse social and cultural components. This is the spirit ingrained in all symbolic struggles between the Harvards and the Yales by whatever names in every time and place.

CHAPTER THREE

Play-Forms
and
Game Principles
as Social
Structures

P revious chapters have established and analyzed the phenomenon of sports and athletics as an essential and constructive dimension in human existence and human experience. This chapter broadens the investigation by relating sports and athletics to the very concepts of society and culture in their origin and manifestation throughout human history. The thesis presented here is that play-forms and game principles reflected in sports and athletics actually shape and mold society and culture and constitute their ideological foundations. This contention reverses the popular assumption that play-forms and game principles (and sports and athletics) *derive* from given societies and cultures and exist as remnants or products of previously established societal structures and cultural orientations. This innovative and controversial theory was proposed originally by Johan Huizinga in his *Homo Ludens*, and developed in greater detail by Roger Caillois in his *Man, Play and Games* (both works are cited earlier).

Work and Play in History and Society

The broader context for this analysis is the basic distinction between play and games and the world of work in our society and culture and in the history of mankind. Especially European and American society have been characterized largely by the "Puritan ethic" or the work ethic which contends that man by nature is a worker and is born to work, and that play and games are an incidental (if not evil) aspect of human experience and should at best be tolerated rather than encouraged. In its ancient and traditional form or interpretation, the substance of the Puritan ethic originates in the biblical story of Genesis and its aftermath—man's "fall from grace in the Garden of Eden" and his subsequent condemnation "to earn his bread by the sweat of his brow." In its modern and contemporary form or interpretation, the Puritan ethic is linked to the Industrial Revolution and mankind's semivoluntary enslavement to material productivity perceived as the key to advanced civilization.

A paradoxical aspect is that the invention of industrial machinery lessened mankind's dependence on his own hands and primitive tools and manual labor in general, and thus set the stage for the development of increased leisure time. This development fructifies in our own times with numerous forms of scientifically advanced industrialization which largely free mankind from much of the drudgery of the work-world. This results in unprecedented expanses of leisure time for the pursuit of personal happiness as opposed to mere survival, and leads to new appreciation for play and games (and sports and athletics) as significant opportunities for the realization of personal self-fulfillment.

These remarks suggest that the nature of play and games and sports and athletics might best be appreciated in the context of the meaning of work and the work world in its basic characteristics. As defined earlier in this study (see chapter I), work is "essentially nonvoluntary human activity pursued in more or less rigidly prescribed socioeconomic contexts in ordinary space and time and involving definite and usually measurable socioeconomic productivity." Play and games are defined as "freely organized and voluntary human activity within its own spatial and temporal boundaries and having its own purposes and rules apart from routine existence and apart from definite and measurable socioeconomic productivity." Sports constitute an extension of play and games characterized by "recognizable degrees of physical exertion and a greater sense of seriousness" compared to play and games. Athletics in turn constitute multisport programs at the amateur, intercollegiate, and professional levels.

Play and Games in Theory and Practice

In contrast to the basic characteristics of the work-world, Huizinga and Caillois contend that play and games (and sports and athletics) constitute another and significantly different realm of being and acting.[1] These authors spell out the distinctions and differences in a list of specific aspects or components of play and games indigenous to these activities and alien to the structure of the work-world. The language describing these play characteristics might vary, but the concepts are consistent and fundamental. Play and games are first of all *free* and *voluntary* and basically spontaneous—they represent things that we *want to do* freely and voluntarily as opposed to things that we *have to do* according to socioeconomic rules for survival. It is incongruous to speak of forced play or forcing someone to play, as exemplified in the contradictory exhortations of harassed parents ordering children "to go out and play and enjoy yourself whether you want to or not." Play and games are *nonproductive* in the socioeconomic sense, and also *nonserious* in this same sense of what must be done to prosper socially and economically.

Especially in professional sports and athletics, and to a large extent in intercollegiate sports and athletics, this sense of seriousness and productivity likens the sports world to the world of work and the distinctions become subtle and analytic. In closely reasoned discussions on this point, Bernard Suits ("The Elements of Sport") and Scott Kretchmar ("Ontological Possibilities: Sport as Play") suggest various significant relationships between play and sport and the seriousness of the work-world. Suits contends that our newfound "leisure ethic" gives sports a special kind of seriousness:

> Sports are precisely like the other interests which occur prominently as leisure activities. They are a type of intrinsic good which, along with many others, makes up the class of goals to which we ascribe that primary seriousness which provides such

things as factories, armies and governments with the derivative seriousness to which they are entitled.[2]

Kretchmar points out that ". . . in playing a ball game an individual's lived experience may be grounded in play one moment and in work the next. Likewise while 'on the job' a person may alternate between playing and working and live the nuances of both."[3]

Huizinga and Caillois further describe play and games as *nonsurvival* in character and separate or apart from ordinary life with its routine cares and anxieties: "play is other-worldly and make-believe." Play and games also occur *in their own space and time* as opposed to routine (work) locales and standard clock and calendar time. Play and games, generally speaking, start and stop at the command of the participants and the directors of the activity, and they have their own locale or their own space and place which is sometimes grandiose, like Olympic sites, and sometimes mundane, like a street corner or someone's backyard. Play and games are literally like productions in a theatre—they take place on their own stage and have their own opening and closing curtains. One of the most eloquent discussions of this special space-time dimension in play and games and sports and athletics occurs in Michael Novak's *The Joy of Sports*, where he contends that ". . .Seven seals lock the inner life of sports (and) they may be broken, one by one." The first two seals are the *Sacred Space* and *Sacred Time* of sports and athletics—the consecrated places and the hallowed moments of sports achievement.

> The feeling athletes have for the arena in which they struggle is a secret feeling not often voiced. If you have ever walked on Paratroopers' Hill in Jerusalem, in the trenches and in the dugouts, recalling the fierce nighttime chaos in the barbed wire where men's bodies were shredded by rockets and automatic weapons, and where the liberation of the city was made possible; or if you have walked the fields of Gettysburg, reconstruct-

ing in imagination the movements and the courage; perhaps then you understand how certain places are hallowed by deeds.

. . .There is a special awe that arises when one enters for the first time—or at any time—one's high school gym, or Madison Square Garden, or Pauley Pavilion, or wherever the symbolic center of achievement may be. Each arena is a little different: one concrete place, one patch of earth, one England. . . .

Sports arenas are storied places. Universes of tales. One sits in them surrounded by ghostly ancestors, as at the Mass one is surrounded by the hosts who have since Abraham celebrated a Eucharist. . .

. . .Where great deeds have been done, places are lifted out of ordinary life and gain a certain aura. It is like that for athletic arenas. Players often feel it. Places where they struggle, where they may suffer injury, where opportunity comes and their careers blossom or, on the other hand, suddenly decline or fail to materialize—places where they meet their trial and testing—have a certain fascination over them. . . .

. . .Arenas are like monasteries; individual games imprint on memory single images blazing as if from an illuminated text. Awesome places, a familiar, quiet sort of awe. Our cathedrals.

. . .(Living the baseball year) is almost like being a Catholic and living according to the calendar of the liturgy, or being Jewish and counting the seasons and years along another axis of memory.

Sacred time is sacred because it stores up possibilities of the heroic; so long as sacred time exists, the heroic is in incubation. Sacred time teaches humans never to quit, to count upon and to entrust themselves to the potencies of life, redemption, beauty. One never knows. Deep in the resources of each of us may be ripening at least one supremely lovely act. . .

Both (sacred) time and the time of the heroes in sports are tokens of eternal life. At moments of high intensity, there seems to be no past, no future. One experiences a complete immersion in the present, absorption in an instantaneous and abundant now. In what seems like an instant, hours of profane time elapse unnoticed. From this experience, the descent into ordinary time is like exchanging one form of life for another. . . .[4]

Huizinga and Caillois assert that the final characteristic of play and games distinguishing them from ordinary life is that they are essentially *rules-governed* with their own statutes and commandments for behavior. These rules make the game what it is by permitting and encouraging participants to perform certain acts and strictly prohibiting contrary forms of behavior within the game. These rules are sometimes involved and complex as in chess and soccer, and sometimes simplistic as in children's games. Whatever else might be involved, there is always the basic rule about play and games (and sports and athletics) that "now we are playing" and then "we are no longer playing." Bernard Suits propounds an unusually scholarly and incisive analysis of the rules factor in play and games and sports and athletics in his *The Grasshopper: Games, Life and Utopia.* He makes the critical observation that "rules in games thus seem to be in some sense inseparable from ends. . . . If the rules are broken the original end becomes impossible of attainment, since one cannot (really) win the game unless he plays it, and one cannot (really) play the game unless he obeys the rules of the game."[5]

Play-Forms and Game Principles

Again the basic purpose of this chapter is to demonstrate the thesis that play-forms and game principles reflected in sports and athletics actually shape and mold society and culture. Caillois introduces the issue in the following comments:

For a long time the study of games has been scarcely more than the history of games. Attention has been focused upon the equipment used in games more than on their nature, character-istics, laws, instinctive basis, or the type of satisfaction that they provide. They have generally been regarded as simple and insignificant pastimes for children. There was no thought of attributing the slightest culture value to them. . . .

Huizinga, however, in his key work *Homo Ludens*. . . defends the very opposite thesis, that culture is derived from play. Play is simultaneously liberty and invention, fantasy and discipline. All important cultural manifestations are based upon it. It creates and sustains the spirit of inquiry, respect for rules, and detachment. In some respects the rules of law, prosody, counterpoint, perspective, stagecraft, liturgy, military tactics, and debate are rules of play. They constitute conventions that must be respected. Their subtle interrelationships are the basis for civilization. In concluding *Homo Ludens*, one asks oneself, 'What are the social consequences of play?'. . . .

In the end, the question of knowing which preceded the other, play or the serious, is a vain one. To explain games as derived from laws, customs, and liturgies, or in reverse to explain jurisprudence, liturgy, and the rules for strategy, syllogisms, or esthetics as a derivation of play, are complementary, equally fruitful operations provided they are not regarded as mutually exclusive. The structures of play and reality are often identical, but the respective activities that they subsume are not reducible to each other in time or place. They always take place in domains that are incompatible. . . .

Inasmuch as I am also convinced that there exist precise interrelationships of compensation or connivance in games, customs, and institutions, it does not seem to me unreasonable to find out whether the very destiny of cultures, their chance to flourish or stagnate, is not equally determined by their preference for one or another of the basic categories into which I have tried to divide games, categories that are not equally creative. In other words, I have not only undertaken a sociology of games, I have the idea of laying the foundations for a sociology *derived from* games.[6]

CLASSIFICATION OF GAME PRINCIPLES

The demonstration of these contentions that play-forms and game principles might well shape the nature of societies and cultures begins with the classification of play and games into four categories with corresponding categorical principles. These four categories with their game principles are: (1) competitive struggle (*agon*); (2) games of chance (*alea*); (3) illusion and imagery (*mimicry*); and (4) equilibrium and alteration (*ilinix* or *vertigo*).[7] It is also possible (though not necessary for the purpose of this discussion) to subdivide each category into free and unstructured play activity (*paidia*) and disciplined or structured play activity (*ludus*).

> I do not intend, in resorting to these strange concepts, to set up some kind of pedantic, totally meaningless mythology. However, obligated as I am to classify diverse games under the same general category, it seemed to me that the most economical means of doing so was to borrow, from one language or another, the most meaningful and comprehensive term possible, so that each category examined should avoid the possibility of lacking the particular quality on the basis of which the unifying concept was chosen.[8]

The first category is competitive struggle or *agon*, best reflected in play and games (and sports and athletics) based on forms of conflict and strife: between teams (football and lacrosse); between individuals (boxing and tennis); or between individuals and nature (golf, skiing, and running). This also includes games such as checkers, chess, billiards, and others in which "the search for equality is so obviously essential to the rivalry that it is re-established by a handicap for players of different classes; that is, within the equality of chances already established, a secondary inequality, proportionate to the relative powers of the participants, is dealt with."[9] The second basic game category and principle is chance or *alea* and this would be play and games (and aspects of sports and athletics) in which there is less emphasis on skilled activity exercised in sporting combat and less control of oneself and nature (dice games, roulette wheels, and lotteries).

Alea signifies and reveals the favor of destiny. The player is entirely passive; he does not deploy his resources, skill, muscles or intelligence. All he need do is await, in hope and trembling, the cast of the die. . . . *Alea* is total disgrace or absolute favor. It grants the lucky player infinitely more than he could procure by a lifetime of labor, discipline and fatigue. It seems an insolent and sovereign insult to merit. . . .[10]

Some forms of play and games (backgammon and sophisticated card games) and most forms of sports and athletics combine *agon* and *alea*, and this is significant in itself and in later aspects of this thesis that sports and athletics constitute the basis of society and culture. It is interesting to observe also that this combination of *agon* and *alea* in sports and athletics is the basis of betting and handicapping, which historically and especially in contemporary society are an integral part of the sporting enterprise: "Assuming that the chances of the competitors are as equal as possible, it follows that every encounter with competitive characteristics and ideal rules can become the object of betting or alea."[11]

The third category and principle of play and games (also reflected in sports and athletics) is illusion and imagery or *mimicry*. This is basically forms of play and games which involve imitation or simulation of other people and other situations, but the concept has a significant and demonstrable role in the very nature of sports and athletics. "All play presupposes the temporary acceptance, if not of an illusion (indeed this last word means nothing less than beginning a game: *inlusio*), then at least of a closed, conventional, and in certain aspects, imaginary universe."[12] In its simplest manifestation or expression as a game principle, *mimicry* is the motivation for children's playful imitation of parents and other authoritarian and romantic figures (including sports heroes), and as such constitutes the ideological foundation for the entire toy industry of tools and machines to imitate adults. In its more sophisticated dimensions as a game principle, *mimicry* is the basis of theatrical productions and dramatic interpretations in the theaters of the world throughout history to our own times.

Mimicry as a game principle is an essential aspect and operative concept in the nature of sports and athletics, since these are fundamentally spectacles and exhibitions whose total integrity involves and requires spectators who are really mimics at heart. "(Sports events) are intrinsic spectacles, with costumes, solemn overture, appropriate liturgy, and regulated procedures. In a word, these are dramas whose vicissitudes keep the public breathless, and lead to denouements which exalt some and depress others."[13] As indicated earlier (see chapter II), sports fans are what they are because they share vicariously in the game or spectacle even to the extent of imitating the participants with their own bodily movements. Especially in younger sports fans, this mimicry-adulation extends to hairstyles and dress codes and the wearing of T-shirts with favored names and numbers, and even to sometimes ill-advised attempts to copy playing styles in various sports. "Identification with the champion in itself constitutes *mimicry* related to that of the reader with the hero of the novel and that of the moviegoer with the film star."[14]

The fourth and final category and principle of play and games is equilibrium and alteration or *vertigo (ilinx)*, and this would be play and games (and sports and athletics) in which there is some attempt to alter and/or control one's physical and mental balance in the world. In its simplest manifestation or expression as a game principle, *vertigo* or *ilinx* characterizes children's games in which they spin around and around either singly or in groups until they are dizzy and giddy, and then delight in the feeling of slow restoration to normal equilibrium. Advanced forms of *vertigo* play and games would be the carnival and circus machinery designed to elaborate and intensify the spinning and the whirling—the ferris wheel and roller-coasters and other contraptions constructed to fling people about in every direction.

Vertigo as a game principle is reflected also in more serious and semimystical religious tribal rites involving wild and protracted bodily gyrations intended to produce trances and stupors and emotional removal from the ordinary world. Somewhat closer to the realm of sports and athletics, *vertigo* as a game principle is the basis for some primitive and dangerous ceremonial play-forms in some tribal societies in different parts of the world. One example is the brutal test of courage and daring in the name of religious values practiced by African tribes, in which participants climb to the top of tall trees and then dive headlong toward the ground, held by vines attached to their ankles and carefully gauged and measured to jerk the diver to a stop just as his head brushes the ground. Caillois refers specifically to the Huastec and Totonac *voladores*, who perform similar ceremonial stunts as the "dance of the setting sun, associated with birds, the deified dead," in which participants swan-dive from tall poles with ropes attached to their bodies and the wings of birds attached to their waists.[15] More conventional forms of sports and athletics reflecting the *vertigo* game principle include skiing, surfing, diving, tight-rope walking, sky diving, gliding, and especially the contemporary fascination with skateboarding as a sporting experience. Caillois summarizes the *vertigo* principle in these comments:

> The last kind of game includes those which are based on the pursuit of vertigo and which consist of an attempt to momentarily destroy the stability of perception and inflict a kind of voluptuous panic upon an otherwise lucid mind. In all cases, it is a question of surrendering to a kind of spasm, seizure or shock which destroys reality with sovereign brusqueness. . . .

> Essential is the pursuit of this special disorder or sudden panic, which defines the term vertigo, and in the true characteristics of the games associated with it: viz., the freedom to accept or refuse the experience, strict and fixed limits, and separation from the rest of reality. What the experience adds to the spectacle does not diminish but reinforces its character as play.[16]

Games and Sports as Dimensions of Society

This classification of play-forms and game principles reflected in sports and athletics is the context for the next step in this thesis that sports and athletics constitute the very basis of society and culture. The pivotal contention is that these four game principles of *agon-alea-mimicry-vertigo* play a definitive role in the nature and development of social organization. The documentation for this contention is that these game principles are: 1) first recognized and acted out in play and games and sports and athletics; 2) eventually reflected in various ways in society and culture; and 3) powerful influences in society and culture including the potentiality for significant forms of social and cultural disruption and corruption. This is depicted in the following schematic pattern of these basic game principles in their nature and consequences.[17]

1. *Agon* (competitive struggle)

   a) first recognized and acted out in games and sports such as football and boxing.
   b) clearly reflected in society and culture in any and every form of social and cultural competition (in business, politics, and education).
   c) has the potential to disrupt and corrupt society and culture in breeding the "will to power" and acts of deceit and violence among competitors intent on winning.

2. *Alea* (confronting the laws of chance)

   a) first recognized and acted out in games and sports such as casino gambling and horse racing.
   b) clearly reflected in society and culture in any and every form of "taking a chance" for progress and profit (Wall Street speculations and state lotteries among other activities).
   c) has the potential to disrupt and corrupt society and

culture in leading to undue emphasis on superstition and astrological and other mystic forces in an attempt to "side with nature."

3. *Mimicry* (illusion and imagination and imitation)

a) first recognized and acted out in various games involving masquerades including theater and drama, and perceived also in the role of sports spectators.

b) clearly reflected in society and culture in various forms of ritual and symbol designed to transport people out of the ordinary world into the unchanging world of ideals and fanciful desires (examples are elusive here—perhaps masquerade balls and parades and various shows of religious and patriotic idealism).

c) has the potential to disrupt and corrupt society and culture in leading to forms of self-alienation and even schizophrenic tendencies.

4. *Vertigo* (*ilinx* or equilibrium and alteration)

a) first recognized and acted out in games and sports such as "the whirling dervish" and gymnastics and pole-vaulting.

b) clearly reflected in society and culture in various attempts to change or alter one's social and cultural status realistically or artifically.

c) has the potential to disrupt and corrupt society and culture in prompting the use of alcohol and drugs as extreme forms of world-alteration.

These contentions indicate that these basic game principles must be regarded as significant elements in determining so many critical dimensions in the nature of social and cultural structure. It is probably surprising and shocking to realize that play-forms and game principles constitute the potential origin of some of our most serious social and cultural maladies: violence, deceit, and superstition; self-alienation and personality disorders; and alcoholism and drug addiction. It should be emphasized that these play-forms and game principles are essentially good and productive in themselves and in society, and the proper and constructive course of action is to avoid and combat the potential for abuse inherent in the situation.

The final argument in this thesis that game principles and sports and athletics characterize society and culture begins with the proper combination of these four principles into two groups or sets of forces. Some combinations are meaningless and even impossible: *agon* and *vertigo* cannot be combined since *agon* is basically structured and *vertigo* is basically unstructured; and *alea* and *mimicry* are contradictory in character. The proper combination of these game principles is the combination of *agon-alea* and the combination of *mimicry-vertigo*. Caillois' social theory of game principles contends that all societies and cultural organizations reflect and adhere to these fundamental combinations of game principles. These are the two sets of structural forces that have shaped and ruled the two generic forms of society and culture throughout human history to the present day.

In this broader historical context of social and cultural development, these fundamental combinations of game principles as structural forces are first recognized in ancient Greek mythology—specifically in the twin personages of the classic gods Dionysus and Apollo. Greek mythological accounts of these divinities describe Dionysus as the god of emotional celebration and the free spirit in life and society, and in contrast Apollo is portrayed as the god of reason and intellect and the orderly and rational mode of life and society. In the context of these combinations of game principles as the basis of society and culture, Dionysus is the god of *mimicry-vertigo* or the god of historical and contemporary primitive and emotionally based societies and cultures. Such societies and cultures are characterized by their attempts to live by imitating and relating to nature in body and mind through rituals and ceremonies, including such activities as sorcery and witchcraft and spirit-presence. Dionysian societies mimic mysterious and powerful "forces of the world," and tend to portray good and evil in personified and priestly aspects and manifestations of nature.

In contrast to this Dionysian (*mimicry-vertigo*) form of society and culture, Apollo is the god of *agon-alea* or the god of rationally oriented and rules-governed societies and cultures in whatever time and whatever place. Apollonian societies and cultures are generally associated with higher levels of civilization and sophistication from the ancient Egyptians and Greeks and Romans down to our own Western world. Our Apollonian society is motivated primarily by meritorious *agon* in the face of chance: we gain merit for ourselves and for others through worthy struggle and competition, but there is always the element of chance laced through the *agon* of our lives.[18]

Specifically in the context of sports and athletics as the basis of society and culture, the *agon-alea* character of our social and cultural structure is clearly indicated in the fact that our society's strongest universal interests and attractions are sports and athletic events based on competition and chance (professional football, hockey, and major intercollegiate sports). For better or for worse, our society is not ballet-oriented or symphony-oriented or museum-oriented. Far more millions of our citizens are devoted to sports and athletics in general, and to such national and traditional spectacles as the World Series, the Super Bowl, and the Rose Bowl. Our society and our culture and our national spirit are the products of the game principles of *agon* and *alea* and their fundamental influence in shaping our life and our times.

CHAPTER FOUR

Existentialism and the Athlete

S cholarly studies of the philosophical and humanistic dimensions in sports and athletics should relate the sporting enterprise to commonly recognized philosophical attitudes and approaches wherever the relationship is valid and logical. This is important in the nature of the studies themselves, and in further illustrating the fundamentally philosophical character of sports and athletics in human existence. This chapter is an introduction to the spirit and premises of existentialist philosophy, and an indication and explication of existentialism's unique and significant influences in the world of sports and athletics.

Existentialism is probably the most popular and most pervasive trend or theme in Western philosophy since its inception in the philosophical teachings of Soren Kierkegaard (1813-55) and Friedrich Nietzsche (1844-1900). The universality of the existentialist approach is apparent in contemporary professional philosophical circles, and also in representative schools of contemporary theology and psychology and in many areas and aspects of European and American literature. Possibly some of the professional and popular interest and enthusiasm relating to existentialism has waned somewhat since the peak of its popularity in the two decades immediately after World War II, but the movement is still evident and significant in scholarship and personal allegiance throughout the Western world.

Existentialism is a philosophical attitude (rather than system or doctrine) whose basic tenet is emphasis on the "primacy and dignity of the human reality as an individual." Existentialism rejects abstract speculations and generalizations about reality and human existence, and focuses on the existence and experiences of the individual and the *hard immediacy* of the present decision as the most meaningful context for knowledge and value. The main frame of reference is always the individual's life and actions as the life is lived through the actions. Existentialism emphasizes the concrete rather than the abstract and the individual rather than the universal, and stresses above all the essential and total freedom and personal subjectivity of the individual in being and acting.

Existentialist Philosophy: Spirit and Character

Existentialism is an intensely personal and individual portrayal of reality and human existence and this can create some difficulties in defining and assessing existentialist philosophy. Several avowed and classic existentialist philosophers reject the term *existentialist* as a label or description of their approach, since this common branding suggests a unity or universality of thought which is contrary to their freedom and individuality of expression. The fundamental polarity in existentialist philosophy is the distinction between atheistic or secular existentialism (Jean-Paul Sartre) and Christian existentialism (Gabriel Marcel and Nicolai Berdyaev), with several variations on these basic themes. Both atheistic and Christian existentialism emphasize individual freedom and subjectivity and the importance of personal choice and values, although the world of the Christian existentialist tends to be more hopeful and more ultimately meaningful since it includes the concept of God and the possibility of eternal salvation beyond the temporal satisfaction of a life well-lived.

Despite the diversity and variety in existentialist philosophy, all such versions reflect or manifest certain common characteristics which give existentialist philosophy its unique character and recognizable form. These characteristics are the following: 1) existentialist philosophy is a *living* or *lived* philosophy rather than a formal or academic philosophy; 2) existentialist philosophy distinguishes *authentic* existence from *inauthentic* existence and stresses the importance of authentic existence; 3) existentialist philosophy emphasizes *consciousness-of-self* and *personal subjectivity*; 4) existentialist philosophy opposes *rationalism* and *intellectualism* as ways of explaining reality and ways of explaining human knowledge; 5) existentialist philosophy is a constant *subjective experience* that can be illustrated but never completely communicated; and 6) existentialist philosophy emphasizes the *plight of the individual* in the world.

To say that existentialist philosophy is a *living* or *lived* philosophy means that its precepts and tenets are embodied in the life and actions of the individual as a conscious participant in existence and experience. Existentialist philosophy is primarily the individual's conscious awareness of one's own being and the dimensions of one's experiences in confronting reality in the world. *Authentic* existence is the individual's conscious recognition (and exploitation) of the definitive aspects of meaningful human existence: absolute freedom and individuality and subjectivity. *Inauthentic* existence is the surrender or the subordination of these aspects to function and utility or to the crowd-mentality and socioreligious and political institutions. *Consciousness-of-self* is an acute and enlightened form of self-consciousness reflected in *subjectivity*, or the awareness of oneself as an original center of free initiative existing in the world as an entity marked with the finitude of death.

Existentialist philosophy opposes *rationalism* and *intellectualism* as modes or ways of knowing because these views conceptualize reality into rigid and abstract patterns, and thus detract from the vibrancy and dynamism and the *hard immediacy* of personal experience in making or creating one's own world. One of the unique aspects of the existentialist approach is its character as a constant *subjective experience* that can be illustrated but never completely communicated. Existentialist philosophy is identified and constituted by the individual's own personal existential experience in being and acting, and thus can never be systematized into principles and premises to be communicated in a pedagogical sense.

The possibility of *illustrating* an existentialist viewpoint or an existentialist experience is the basis of literary existentialism, in which life and experience are depicted from an existentialist perspective within the context of fictional or semifictional situations. The *plight of the individual* in existentialist philosophy refers to the frequently awesome awareness of the human condition reflected in our lives as entities "abandoned in the world" with nothing and no one to guide us: we are left to our own personal choices and decisions and the immense responsibility for our own existential destiny. As indicated earlier in the comparison between atheistic and Christian existentialism, the plight of the individual in Christian existentialism is ameliorated somewhat through the consolation of spiritual relationships.

Existentialist philosophy is largely identified in the popular mind with the life and writings of Jean-Paul Sartre (1905-80), and classic formulations are propounded also in the works of Gabriel Marcel (1889-1973) and Martin Heidegger (1889-1976). Other leading existentialist philosophers include Karl Jaspers and Maurice Merleau-Ponty, and the Spaniards Miguel de Unamuno and Jose Ortega y Gassett. Existentialist theology is portrayed in the religious views of Nicolai Berdyaev, Paul Tillich, and Martin Buber. Literary existentialism is reflected in contemporary authors including Albert Camus, Simone de Beauvoir, Fyodor Dostoyevsky, and Herman Hesse. Much interesting and significant pioneer research in existential psychoanalysis is contributed by Rollo May and Victor Frankl.

Scholarly explications and critiques of existentialist philosophy are extensive in number and diversified in character. The definitive expressions of existentialist philosophy are Sartre's *Being and Nothingness* (1956) and Marcel's *The Mystery of Being* (1950), and in certain areas Heidegger's *Being and Time* (1962). Classic secondary sources include W.C. Barrett's *Irrational Man* (1958); H.J. Blackham's *Six Existentialist Thinkers* (1952); James Collins' *The Existentialists* (1952); F.C. Copleston's *Existentialism and Modern Man* (1948); Wilfred Desan's *The Tragic Finale*

(1954); Marjorie Grene's *Dreadful Freedom* (1948); and Jean Wahl's *A Short History of Existentialism* (1949). See also this writer's *Existentialism and Thomism* (1969).[1]

Existentialism and the Athlete

Existentialism in sports and athletics centers on the concept of the athlete as an individual in the world who is acutely aware of the significance of concrete and personal experience, and who is intensely committed to personal values and goals for the moment and for one's athletic lifetime. The athlete reflects an integral unity of consciousness and bodily presence in the world, directed to the achievement of specific purposes "here and now" and apart from speculations and abstractions. The athlete is measured by actions and deeds actually performed now and forever and never by intentions and idealizations that exist only in the realm of the mind. In the philosophically perceptive study *The Philosophic Process in Physical Education*, it is observed that ". . . There are excellent illustrations in sports of man's long history (pre-Homer) of the human expectation that the individual performer is responsible for what he does. Simonodis and, before him, Hesoid in their poems both point out this same theme. That is, before man expressed the individual's responsibility, he practiced it."[2]

In the unity of consciousness and bodily presence in the lived experience of sports and athletics, the athlete represents the total person experiencing oneself and the world as an authentic and truly committed individual in the existentialist context. Sports and athletics reflect existentialism's rejection of mind-body dualism and its emphasis on our unity and identity as consciousness-in-the-world-with-a-body. Mind-body dualism is an aspect of various philosophical systems and attitudes in the history of philosophy (notably Rene Descartes' radical dualism of *thought* and *extension*), and tends to portray the body as an object distinct from the mind and "out there" in the world. This portrayal of the body as an object somehow distinct from the mind has serious and diverse philosophical and humanistic consequences, and among other things constitutes the basis for various hedonistic and sexist attitudes including our contemporary Playboy (and Playgirl) philosophies. When the body is perceived as an object in the world, one's own body and the bodies of others can be perceived as possessions and instruments to be used for various (pleasure) purposes—usually resulting in the degradation of dignity and virtue. Sports and athletics are directed by their nature and purpose to the achievement of human excellence at the physical level, and thus the athlete is the model of personal consciousness and bodily presence in the world as an integrated entity in being and acting.

In the interests of accuracy and scholarship, it must be noted that the concept of the *body* and bodily presence in the world constitute a serious problem for some existentialist thinkers in their analysis of human existence. This is especially true in Jean-Paul Sartre's definitive version of existentialist philosophy; his attempts to deal with "The Problem of the Body" (and "The Problem of the Other" who perceives my body) are discussed at length throughout the second part of his 722-page *Being and Nothingness*.[3] The problem is that existentialist philosophy (especially Sartre's existentialism) defines the human reality primarily as *consciousness* or conscious subjectivity, perceived as essentially nonphysical in nature and character. One of the basic reasons for this view is to guarantee the ontological freedom of the human reality as a "translucid and non-substantial" entity, totally free and unbounded by physical dimensions and limitations. Obviously the presence of the body as a physically bounded and determined aspect of human existence interferes with this nonphysical concept of the human reality and human freedom, and creates ideological anguish and conflict in the existential analysis of mankind.

Despite these theoretical and conceptual difficulties, existentialist philosophers are compelled in various ways to accept the fact of the body, and this is generally expressed in some version of the notion that "consciousness-exists-a-body" and is located in the spatial-temporal world. Gabriel Marcel's Christian existentialism speaks more poetically of the human reality as "incarnated spirit" or spiritual consciousness incarnated in the body, with all the symbolism and significance of the religious Incarnation of Jesus Christ. Thus it is legitimate and realistic to describe the existential human reality as consciousness-in-the-world-with-a-body with all that this entails and portends for sports and athletics and the athletes of the world.

This contention that athletes are existential realities *par excellence* relates especially to one of existentialism's most significant precepts, and this is once again the importance of self-identity and personal integrity achieved through lived experience or the experiential intuition of oneself and reality. The significance of this is that such individual immersion in one's world precludes and eliminates tendencies toward self-alienation and alienation from the world. Self-alienation and alienation from the world result from lack of personal authenticity and probity, and a sense of being somehow separate and apart from the world rather than *creating* one's world through subjective choices and decisions and heroic actions. This separation from oneself and the world brings about a kind of *malaise* in the human condition, and leads to the *bad faith* or personal dishonesty and self-deception so despised in the existential ideal of human existence. The athlete's acute consciousness of self as a functioning bodily presence in the immediate world of personal experience is the source of self-affirmation and the basis for authentic oneness with the world.

One of the subtle paradoxes in analyzing the existential aspects of sports and athletics is that *thinking* about (the athlete's) bodily presence in the world often distorts this presence and detracts from its integrity and validity. This relates in some respects to previous comments to the effect that existentialist philosophy rejects rationalism and intellectualism—primarily because such views conceptualize and idealize reality and human existence, and thus nullify the vibrancy and dynamism of the confrontational experience. The point is that sports and athletics subsume an artistry of consciousness and bodily presence that must be perceived in terms of lived experience rather than conceptual analysis. There is a spontaneity and inventiveness (without arbitrariness) in existential being and acting, and there is a similar spontaneity and inventiveness (without arbitrariness) in sports and athletics and the athlete's being and acting. This is much more than mere instinctive actions and reactions: it is the measure once again of the existential athlete's attunement with the experiential world.

The existential athlete does not *think* about space and time in the world—the athlete *lives* space and time in the world in his or her uniquely acute expression of consciousness-in-the-world-with-a-body. A good example is the anecdote about Yogi Berra used to begin this book. When Yogi contended that "he couldn't think and hit at the same time—it's got to be one or the other," he epitomized the distinction between conceptual analysis and existential action in specific human situations. Conceptual analysis tends to "freeze" reality into static moments of thought and intention, rather than dynamic choices and decisions engendering in successful action. Thinking about hitting is important but only as a kind of prelude destined to be translated into action suited to the hard immediacy of the moment. A more sophisticated and more philosophical explanation of the same phenomenon occurs in John McPhee's *A Sense of Where You Are: A Profile of William Warren Bradley* (1965).[4] Bill Bradley was an All-American basketball player at Princeton, and extended his distinguished scholastic career as a Rhodes Scholar at Cambridge before playing professional basketball and eventually entering politics as a U.S. Senator from New Jersey.

McPhee's thematic interview with Bradley took place on the basketball court during a practice session, and while they talked the player moved through a series of self-devised shooting drills. As McPhee watched Bradley execute a certain shot time after time and seemingly from exactly the same spot on the court, he asked him how he knew when and where to let the shot go to achieve maximum results. Bradley replied that he had previously measured and mapped out the whole maneuver, and knew that he had to be positioned a certain distance from the sideline and a certain distance from the baseline and had to assume a certain angle to the basket. The journalist remarked that during a fast-paced game "you certainly can't stop and decide whether you are a certain number of feet from the sideline and the baseline and so on," and Bradley replied that in (the existential activity of) the game "you have to have *a sense of where are are* and what you can do." In an implicit statement of existentialist attitudes about being and acting, Bradley extends this insight to life in general and our need to be naturally aware without constant analysis of where we are and what we can do in being and acting.

Sports and Zen Philosophies

A different and intriguing approach to the nonconceptual dimensions of sports and athletic participation is reflected in sporadic but enthusiastic accounts of Zen philosophies and other forms of Eastern mysticism applied to the sporting enterprise. The substance of this approach is that properly oriented athletes can achieve surprisingly successful results by eliminating the mind and ego-consciousness from their physical performance, and withdrawing into a mystical state in which the body is "let go" to function as an entity in itself. An interesting and authoritative discussion of these possibilities is contained in "Sport is a Western Yoga" in Adam Smith's *Powers of Mind* (1975).[5] This study suggests that "to groove your game, you have to play without your mind," and quotes a Zen tennis master asserting that . .

> The right shot at the right moment does not come because you do not let go of yourself. . .the right art is purposeless, aimless!

What stands in your way is that you have a much too willful will. You think what you do not do yourself does not happen.[6]

The article attributes Jack Nicklaus' legendary golfing success to his immense powers of concentration which enable him "to play in a trance,. . .he and the club and the ball are all the same thing and there isn't anything else. He can lock right in, real one-pointedness. I think he can influence the flight of the ball even after it's hit."[7] Similar experiences are cited in the athletic career of John Brodie, former star professional football quarterback and now a sports commentator, who contends that. . .

> The player can't be worrying about the past or the future, or the crowd or some other extraneous event. He must be able to respond in the here and now. . .At times, I experience a kind of clarity that I've never seen described in any football story; sometimes this seems to slow way down, as if everyone were moving in slow motion. It seems as if I have all the time in world to watch the receivers run their patterns, and yet I know the defensive line is coming at me just as fast as ever, and yet the whole thing seems like a movie or a dance in slow motion. It's beautiful.[8]

Existentialism and Sports: Classical Theories

One of the most authoritative existentialist inquiries into the essential nature of play and games (and sports and athletics) is developed at length in Sartre's *Being and Nothingness*, specifically in the section on "Existential Psychoanalysis" which includes "The Problem of the Body." The central theme throughout Sartre's existentialist philosophy is the theme of human freedom, which he perceives as total and absolute: "To be human is to be free and to be free is to be human." This is the theme that he perceives clearly in play and games and sports and athletics, and this is the measure of the play-world's fundamental reality and authenticity. Mankind committed to the serious work-world is not free; only man at play is free—free to be creative and innovative and free to establish rules and principles for being and doing.

> There remains one type of activity which we willingly admit is entirely gratuitous: the activity of *play* and the 'drives' which relate back to it. Can we discover an appropriate drive in sport? To be sure, it must be noted first that play as contrasted with the spirit of seriousness appears to be the least possessive attitude; it strips the real of its reality. The serious attitude involves starting from the world and attributing more reality to the world than to oneself; at the very least the serious man confers reality on himself to the degree to which he belongs to the world. . . .All serious thought is thickened by the world; it coagulates; it is a dismissal of human reality in favor of the world. The serious man is 'of the world' and has no resource in himself. He does not even imagine any longer the possibility of *getting out* of the world, for he has given to himself the type of existence of the rock, the consistency, the inertia, the opacity of being-in-the-midst-of-the-world. It is obvious that the serious man at bottom is hiding from himself the consciousness of his freedoms; he is in *bad faith* and his bad faith aims at presenting himself to his own eyes as a consequence; everything is a consequence for him, and there is never any beginning. . . .
>
> Play, like Kierkegaard's irony, releases subjectivity. What is play indeed if not an activity of which man is the first origin, for which man himself sets the rules, and which has no consequence except according to the rules posted? As soon as a man apprehends himself as free and wishes to use his freedom. . .then his activity is play. The first principle of play is man himself; through it he escapes his natural nature; he himself sets the value and rules for his acts and consents to play only according to the rules which he himself has established and defined. . . .[9]

These remarks identify and summarize Sartre's interpetations of the cardinal human failure, and this is the rejection or the denial of human freedom as the essence of human reality. The absolute character of human freedom is awesome to behold and terrifying to accept for some human realities, primarily because such absolute personal freedom brings with it absolute personal responsibility for being and acting. Some people attempt to flee from this "dreadful freedom" and seek to escape it by taking refuge in the seriousness of the work-world or in the bosom of sociopolitical and religious institutions. This denial of human freedom is perforce the denial of authentic human existence, and thus, such human realities exist inauthentically and in *bad faith* as part of the world of objects and things (*being-in-itself*). Play and games (and sports and athletics) are ennobled because they originate and guarantee human freedom, and provide means and opportunities to avoid the self-alienation that comes with turning away from our freedom and subjectivity.

The fundamental and far-reaching significance of Sartre's existentialist views on play and sport is his contention that the play-world represents the essentially real world—the world of what we *are* and should *be* as free and conscious existents. In many ways this is the total statement about the nature and destiny of human existence.

> The point of these remarks, however, is not to show us that in play the desire to *do* is irreducible. On the contrary we must conclude that the desire to do is here reduced to a certain desire to be. The act is not its own goal for itself; neither does its explicit end represent its goal and its profound meaning; but the function of the act is to make manifest and to present to *itself* the absolute freedom which is the very being of the person. This particular type of project, which has freedom for its foundation and its goals, deserves a special study. . . .It would be necessary to explain in full detail its relations with the project of being-God, which has appeared to us as the deep-seated structure of human reality. (Such a study) belongs rather to an *Ethics*. . .and it supposes in addition taking a position which can be *moral* only in the face of values which haunt the For-itself. Nevertheless the fact remains that the desire to play is fundamentally the desire to be.[10]

For a scholarly study of these aspects of Sartre's critical

analysis of play and sports, see Ralph Netzky's "Playful Freedom: Sartre's Ontology Re-appraised" (Summer 1974). [11]

Earlier existentially oriented views on the relationship of "playful freedom" and the nature of human existence are reflected in the philosophy of Friedrich Nietzsche (1844-1900),who along with Soren Kierkegaard (1813-55) initiates the basic themes and general context for contemporary existentialism. Nietzsche's contention that "God is dead" signifies the demise of the Greco-Christian era with its values and attitudes, and in a similar vein signals the end of the Apollonian tradition and the rebirth of the Dionysian tradition with all that this entails and portends for human civilization (see chapter III). Nietzsche's fundamental premise is that the death of God means that mankind is essentially and absolutely free, and this freedom is perhaps best indicated in the playful and sporting tendencies in human existence.

Nietzsche's "God is dead" thesis is established in a curious way in an episode in his significantly titled and often-quoted *Joyful Wisdom*. [12] The episode depicts a madman running into the market-square of a town shouting to the people that "God is dead!" and then paradoxically the madman goes off to the nearest church and prays. This has led to some confusion and speculation about the real meaning of Nietzsche's dramatic contention about God, but the consensus seems to be that Nietzsche is proclaiming the death of the God of reason, rationality, and metaphysics, the death of the God of the Bible and the entire Greco-Christian and Apollonian tradition. Nietzsche's death of God prepares the way for the emergence of his free and joyful Dionysian society and civilization, in which again forms of play and games and sports and athletics constitute definitive dimensions in human existence.

Along with this theme of joyful freedom leading to true wisdom, other basic themes in Nietzsche's philosophy are the importance of *self-affirmation* and the nature of human life as an unparalleled "tragic celebration." The tragic character or the tragedy of human life is essential because tragedy is the origin of heroism, and the heroic life is the only life in Nietzsche's view (which again relates easily to games and sports and athletics). The heroic conquering of life through "the will to power" is, in turn, cause for joyous celebration as the ultimate expression of the human spirit. This is exemplified in another episode in Nietzsche's work, in which he describes the tragic death of a tight-rope walker who falls from the wire and is killed at the feet of the spectators who were watching. One of the spectators is so moved by the performer's courage and heroism and the tragic moment that he insists on digging a grave for the fallen hero with his bare hands. Life is the joyful and grateful celebration of heroic attempts to dominate and control the tragic possibilities in human existence.

After the death of God thesis, Nietzsche's most popular philosophical theme is the concept of the "superman or overman or *übermensch*"—the new breed of philosopher who rises from the death of God and the ashes of the Greco-Christian and Apollonian traditions to lead mankind to the new life of joyful freedom. The superman is superior intellectually and biologically ("blond and blue-eyed and Aryan"), but most importantly he is superior in his recognition and exploitation of the "will to power" as the basis for the radical transformation of society and civilization. The superman is the crux and the symbolic figure in Nietzsche's famous "transvaluation of values" theory, in which the values and morals of the Greco-Christian tradition are totally rejected and replaced by the single standard of power for its own sake. In his *Genealogy of Morals*, Nietzsche proclaims that the insipid "slave-morality and herd-morality" of the Greeks and Christians is inimical and self-defeating, and insists that mankind must go *Beyond Good and Evil* and live according to the single moral precept that "power is always and naturally good and weakness is always and naturally evil."[13]

The superman is the human figure with the courage and the strength and the boldness to lead such a moral revolution and to inspire mankind to forsake the fetid darkness of traditional ethics and "to look up at the sun" and bravely rise above the old life of slavish compliance to the new life of joyful freedom. Nietzsche's emphasis on play as the symbol and the context of human freedom and the new life climaxes in the figure of the superman, and suggests that the realm of play and games and sports and athletics is the real domain of the superman and the measure of human perfection and aspirations. In the context of Nietzsche's theories and views on the meaning and purpose of human existence, it is tempting to suggest that the world of joyful freedom and the heroic role of the superman are perhaps best symbolized in the world of sports and athletics and the heroic triumphs of the serious athlete.

Soren Kierkegaard's existentially oriented philosophy is less obviously related to play and games and sports and athletics, but there is one area of his thought that provides an interesting basis for a comparison of athletes and existential attitudes in life and experience. Kierkegaard first originates the existential themes of individuality and subjectivity in the religious context of mankind's search for a meaningful God. Kierkegaard was a religious and God-oriented person in his own right, but he was also a classic foe of organized and institutionalized religious views. He asserted simply but significantly that religion "is a matter of the heart" rather than the mind, and insisted that authentic religious fervor is subjectively and individually experienced in a dogmatically blind "leap of faith" that transcends rational attitudes and institutional boundaries. This reflects the essentially existentialist character of his thought: every human reality must personally choose and decide and act alone and apart from institutions in the religious area and in every area of human experience.

Kierkegaard dramatically depicts this fundamental need for personal choice in his *Either/Or*, in which he reduces human existence to everyman's decision *either* to live and function as a freely committed and personally responsible individual *or* to live and function inauthentically in the impersonal facade of institutions and organizations. [14] One of the most popular sequences in this discussion is Kierkegaard's schemata of the "three stages of life" or three ways of living the existential truth. These three stages are: (1) the aesthetic stage; (2) the ethical stage; and (3) the religious stage.

The *aesthetic* way of life represents the existentialist person (committed to individual freedom and personal choices), who exists and acts for given moments and given desires with no intention and no purpose to establish lasting values or standards for oneself or for others. Kierkegaard portrays the aesthetic person (in *Either/Or*) in the character of Don Juan, a sensual young man who freely chooses to seduce a female stranger whom he sees one day walking on a street near his home. He sets up an elaborate and time-consuming plan with the singular purpose and goal of seducing the young woman—simply for the pleasure of the seduction moment with no sense of commitment or responsibility beyond the act itself. After months of carefully planned movements and arrangements, he eventually succeeds and then simply walks away from the act with never a backward glance or thought.

The *ethical* way of life represents the existentialist person (committed to individual freedom and personal choices), who exercises the existentialist spirit *within the system* and through personal involvement in the system. Here there is the sense of lasting values and commitment to oneself and to others, but always within the context and the structure of the system. Kierkegaard portrays the ethical person in the character of Judge Wilhelm, whose philosophy is that "one does what one can" within the system.

The *religious* way of life represents the existentialist person (committed to individual freedom and personal choices) who lives the heroic life and performs heroic actions, and whose life and actions have meaning and significance and lasting value far beyond the man and his times. Few people ever achieve this religious way of life, and Kierkegaard uses as an example the lofty figure of the biblical Abraham ready to sacrifice his beloved son in a high moment of heroic commitment to everlasting truth and value.

An intriguing application of these stages to the world of

sports and athletics is suggested by John A. Doody, director of the honors program and a member of the philosophy faculty at Villanova University, Villanova, Pa. Doody introduced courses in the philosophy of sports into the university curriculum, and created and hosted a television series on the subject ("Fact or Fiction") originating in 1977 from CBS's Philadelphia affiliate. The application is subject to personal preferences and choices with respect to specific sports figures assigned to the three stages.[15]

Religious figures in sports and athletics past and present are the true champions of the game whose superior ability and dedication and charisma enable them to transcend themselves and their own era to serve as a lasting symbol of the sporting enterprise. Examples in this category might include Knute Rockne, Babe Ruth, Babe Didrikson Zaharias, Bobby Jones, Bill Tilden, Joe Louis, Joe DiMaggio, Arnold Palmer, Jack Nicklaus, Muhammed Ali, Vince Lombardi, Bobby Orr, Joe Namath, Pele, and Pete Rose. Ethical figures would be gifted but largely unsung heroes whose dedication to the system of "team play" is their greatest strength and finest triumph. Examples in this category might include Lou Gehrig, Bobby Clarke, Bill Russell, Roberto Clemente, Bill Bradley, Robin Roberts, and all the centers and guards in football, and all the members of championship crew teams in the history of the sport.

Aesthetic figures in sports and athletics would be the star performers who are neither existentially religious or ethical, exceptional athletes and prideful individuals whose dedication is turned inward and who lack the last fine measure of charisma and symbolism. Discretion discourages the citing of specific examples.

CHAPTER FIVE

Collegiate Student-Athletes: Serving Two Masters

I t has been established throughout this study that sports and athletics historically constitute one of the most basic and most universal forms of human interest and human activity, and more specifically constitute an essential and constructive dimension of educational and social development at every stage and especially in higher education. The basic reasons for these contentions are developed in chapter II, and center on the notion that sports and athletics provide the greatest opportunity for the greatest number of people to achieve and to witness human excellence. This argument relates easily and naturally to the case for intercollegiate sports and athletic programs, since the classical purpose and the business of colleges and universities is to encourage and produce human excellence in every form. Intercollegiate sports and athletic programs are probably the most popular and also the most controversial area in the contemporary sports scene, and vociferous debates are waged constantly about the true nature and purpose of intercollegiate sports programs in the context of the pursuit of higher education. As in every other area of sports and athletics, intercollegiate sports and athletics have the powerful potential to produce human excellence and also the disastrous potential for abuse and corruption. The latter potential is particularly disturbing in intercollegiate sports and athletics, since it involves the scarring of lofty educational ideals and the betrayal of sacred trusts ingrained in the guiding institutions of civilization.

This chapter and the following two chapters address some of the controversial issues of intercollegiate sports and athletics, with special focus on the intercollegiate student-athlete as the central figure in much of the controversy. The first part of the discussion deals with some of the theoretical and practical purposes and problems in the life and times of intercollegiate student-athletes, followed by recommendations relating to the nature and importance of institutional responsibility for student-athletes. The third chapter in the series broadens the scope somewhat in discussing theories of winning and competition in intercollegiate sports and athletics and throughout the historical sporting enterprise. This is another much-debated aspect of intercollegiate sports and athletics and other areas of sports participation (and perhaps especially children's sports and athletics): whether the values and purposes of sports and athletics can be achieved merely through competing or contending well, or whether the achievement of human excellence occurs only in the context of winning and the thrill of victory.

Intercollegiate Programs in the Educational Experience

The rationale for intercollegiate sports and athletics and intercollegiate student-athletes originates in the contention proposed and developed throughout this study: the traditional and firmly established recognition of sports and athletics as an integral and constructive dimension of educational and social development especially at the college level. Colleges and universities recognize the values and the contributions of sports and athletics in the *total* college experience of students and alumni, and in the progress and well-being of the institution itself. The typical college with an established varsity sports program for the past fifty years describes its views on intercollegiate athletics in the following statements:

> The College believes that organized intercollegiate and intramural sports programs and free physical activities are an integral part of the college experience.
> The College believes that in keeping with its commitment to the education of the whole person it should provide opportunities for sports participation and witnessing.
> The College believes that in a society where athletics plays such an integral role the publicity generated by our various athletic programs does much to bring the name of the College before the public.

Participation in athletic activities and witnessing such activities are viewed as contributing to the well-being and development of the individual, as well as fostering a sense of belonging to the College community.[1]

A senior administrator at the college elaborates these statements in contending that:

An intercollegiate athletic program contributes to the personal development of those who participate and witness, and the kind of development fostered by such activities overlaps with the kind of development that the College hopes to foster through its academic and other programs:

1. Learning the importance of preparation to achieve goals.
2. Learning to abide by rules.
3. Learning how to delay the need for immediate gratification for the sake of long-range objectives.
4. Learning how to work in collaboration with others while also perfecting one's own individual skills.
5. Learning about one's own capacities and limits (physical and emotional, motivational and intellectual) in practices and contests where feedback tends to be clear and prompt.

A college that offers a rounded program of intercollegiate athletics is a significantly more attractive place to prospective students, has a better chance of retaining students it admits, and increases the likelihood that alumni will maintain their allegiance to the school. The quality of a college's intercollegiate program either enhances or diminishes the institution as a whole.[2]

In a review article assessing the values of intercollegiate athletics (in *Journal of the Philosophy of Sports*, 1979), sports philosopher and *Journal* editor Klaus V. Meier refers to "the possibilities of perceiving sports and athletics as true educational components of the liberal arts program, serving as important forums for the growth of the student (leading to) the incorporation of both procedural and propositional knowledge, of new perceptions and awareness of self, and of the development of personal identity elicited during engagement of sport."[3] Many such testimonials exist extolling the virtues of intercollegiate sports and athletics, and this despite the unfortunate but consistent instances of deplorable malpractices in some intercollegiate sports programs discussed in these chapters. In *Sports in America*, James Michener quotes a letter from George H. Hanford, serving as executive vicepresident of the prestigious College Entrance Examination Board of Princeton, who prepared a scholarly and comprehensive study of intercollegiate sports and athletics (*An Inquiry into the Need for and Feasibility of a National Study of Intercollegiate Athletics*):

> I do not side with those who claim that the negative effects of unethical practices in intercollegiate athletics outweigh the positive values. There is an infection, and because it could spread, something needs to be done to control it. On balance, however, I believe that there is much more that is healthy about intercollegiate athletics than is sick.[4]

Student-Athletes: Opportunities for Success

This chapter is an evaluation of one of the most critical and most basic factors in intercollegiate athletics: the opportunities and motivation for successful academic performance by intercollegiate student-athletes compared to nonathlete students in typical campus settings. This analysis proceeds from two basic premises about student-athletes and higher education in academically sincere colleges and universities. The first premise is that every self-respecting college and university should regard student-athletes as students first and athletes second, and should be genuinely committed to the academic progress and timely graduation of student-athletes as the first priority. Colleges and universities must be keenly aware that the main business of such institutions is to develop the mind of all students and not just their bodies in the interests of athletic achievement.

⊙ The second basic premise is that intercollegiate student-athletes experience real and unique physical and psychological pressures and unusual demands on their time and energy, and these must be considered by the administration and faculty in the interests of justice to all students and to the institution itself. These pressures and demands vary in intensity depending on the nature and extent of athletic involvement by the individual student athlete. Student-athletes involved in serious National Collegiate Athletic Association (NCAA) or Association for Intercollegiate Athletics for Women (AIAW) Division I competition in major sports are naturally more burdened than student-athletes in less competitive programs requiring less time and fewer persistent pressures. Academically sincere colleges and universities should establish athletic policies that are carefully consistent with NCAA and AIAW regulations and recommendations, and also with the practices and rules of the athletic conferences and leagues in which they compete.[5]

The broader context for this discussion is that intercollegiate student-athletes at typical institutions constitute just one of several identifiable categories of students on campus with unique abilities or histories which set them apart from the rest of the student body. Because of these distinctive abilities or histories, these categories of students sometimes require and receive certain considerations in their academic life not necessarily required by other students—although they may be available to all students in a variety of ways. These considerations tend to center on special counseling and tutorial opportunities, but they often extend to different or more flexible admissions standards and more interpretive academic procedures compared to the routine for the rest of the student population (more freedom in registering and course selection and some aspects of grading policies among other things).

In addition to student-athletes, typical examples of special interest groups in most colleges and universities would be educationally and socially underprivileged minority students; special programs for continuing education students (older students and students whose academic careers have been interrupted); honors program students; military veteran students; faculty dependent students (spouses and children); and always the special interest cases involving relatives and friends of the administrative hierarchy and faculty. While the comparison may be less than exact in every respect, some mention might be made of handicapped students and expanding institutional concern to accommodate this minority's special needs physically and academically.

The Plight of the Student-Athlete

Keeping in mind the distinction drawn earlier regarding levels of seriousness and intensity in athletic involvement by individual student-athletes, the plight of the intercollegiate student-athlete is easily depicted. Compared to nonathlete students, the serious student-athlete has two sets of responsibilities and obligations and two sets of goals and objectives. Student-athletes are required and expected to succeed academically and athletically, and the dual requirements naturally intensify and often complicate the normal routine of the college experience. These dual requirements subject student-athletes to two sets of taskmasters vying for their undivided time and attention; two sets of priorities vying for their finite time and energy; and two sets of possibilities for success and failure with all the attendant anxieties, persistent hopes, and natural fears.

Serious intercollegiate student-athletes are pressured physically by demanding and often extended practices and contests, and pressured psychologically in many ways including required absences from class and lack of free time to complete routine classroom assignments and other academic obligations. Perhaps the greatest pressure of all in the college life of student-athletes is the total inflexibility of athletic participation—practices and contests and the need for physical and mental readiness occur on a relentless daily schedule that lasts for months and exists always in the recesses of consciousness. Many student-athletes have commented about this aspect in various publications, and a good first-hand summary is contained in a two-part series written by Barnett Wright in *The Temple Daily News* (30–31 October 1979).[6] In contrast with the situation of the serious student-athlete, the college life of the nonathlete student with a single set of goals and objectives is normally less pressured and generally more flexible in terms of time and freedom for successful academic performance. Certainly there are problems and tensions in the life of nonathlete students (especially those who must work to obtain funds for tuition and support), but normally these students have the benefit of more numerous options and more flexibility in their time and energy schedule.

One common rejoinder to these contentions is that intercollegiate student-athletes are adequately reimbursed for their time and troubles through athletic grants-in-aid providing tuition, room and board, and books in whole or in part. It is true that athletic grants-in-aid are an accepted and integral part of the athletic structure for most student-athletes at most institutions, but the very nature of this contractual agreement leads to the pressures and demands on student-athletes already delineated. Intercollegiate student-athletes on grants are required to perform services for the institution on a *quid pro quo* basis, and the pact is for the mutual benefit of student-athletes and the institution itself. The rationale for athletic grants-in-aid is that student-athletes make contributions to the college now and into the future generally unmatched by the activities of most nonathlete students. One notable comparison might be made between student-athletes adding to the image of the school, and student winners of prestigious academic awards and grants which redound to the credit of the institution (most of whom represent an honors program background with all the rights and privileges thereunto appertaining).

Athletic grants-in-aid constitute a controversial issue in

many respects. Some institutions insist that all grants must be based on financial need alone with no regard for any special abilities in athletics or academics. This was the major issue hotly debated in the 1976 NCAA national convention in St. Louis, and the proposal to base all grants on financial need alone was defeated in a vote representing some 800-member institutions.[7] The main area of opposition then and now is the flexibility of interpretation by individual institutions as to what constitutes financial need and the resultant potential for abuse. NCAA Division III institutions (and some individual conferences—notably the Ivy League) reject athletic grants and base all grants on financial need alone. Many institutions are selective in their policy, and require participants in some sports to submit financial aid statements while exempting participants in major sports programs as an inducement in recruiting blue-chip prospects for such programs.

Serious intercollegiate student-athletes tend to be troubled figures from the very beginning of their college careers. Usually they come to college from a distinguished high school athletic career including special recognition by the student body and the administration and faculty. Usually they have been highly recruited with standard recruiting techniques centering on their superior athletic abilities and their uniqueness among their peers. This often leads to a rude awakening for many freshman student-athletes, who suddenly find they are only one of several equally distinguished and accomplished former high school athletes destined to compete intensely with one another for continued athletic acceptance and recognition. Simultaneously they are confronted with academic procedures requiring much more initiative and self-reliance compared to high school, and the expectation to perform more effectively in the classroom than ever before. Much of this is part of the routine initiation to the demands of college life, but the situation is significantly compounded for most student-athletes compared to nonathlete students. Some of this pressure might be alleviated if freshman were ineligible to compete in varsity sports, but the demands and ambitions of major college sports programs make restoration of the freshman ineligibility rule something of a lost cause.[8]

Intercollegiate student-athletes very often are subjected to bias and prejudice from various segments of the college community especially the student body and faculty. They tend to be stereotyped in their interests, intellectual ability, and ambition, and they are often associated with an "elitist syndrome" in which they are perceived to regard themselves as different and superior to the rest of the student population. Probably the only type of comment that can be offered is that bias and prejudice undeniably exist in various forms as deficiencies in the human spirit, and that unsupportable generalizations and dubious sterotyping are as inaccurate about intercollegiate student-athletes as any other segment of the college community or society in general. An interesting psychological summary of these campus perceptions about student-athletes with recommendations for coping is contained in Ron Tongate's article, "Athletes: Counseling the Overprivileged Minority," (June 1978).[9]

Some special comments should be added about the compounded plight of increasing numbers of female intercollegiate student-athletes in the wake of Title IX legislation and increased social consciousness for sexual equality.[10] Especially in colleges and universities which turn coeducational from all-male student bodies (notably some of the Ivy League institutions), female students sometimes encounter overt and subtle opposition in their rightful efforts to be recognized as persons and as academically qualified and purposeful individuals. Female intercollegiate student-athletes face the added burden of establishing recognition and acceptance as serious and accomplished athletes. Extensive female participation in organized intercollegiate and professional athletics is relatively recent in origin (the AIAW was founded in 1970), and female athletes still encounter lingering suspicion and cultural opposition in their desire to combine athletic participation and feminine respectability.

Staunch ERA advocates and some interpretations of Title IX would quickly supply definitive and comprehensive responses to such attitudes, but in the meantime, female intercollegiate student-athletes are left to confront the inequity, patronizing, and indifference they often receive on campuses throughout the nation. Several lawsuits have already been filed by female student-athletes at various institutions alleging sex discrimination between male and female sports programs in financial and other areas protected by Title IX provisions. The basic principle is that female intercollegiate student-athletes want to be perceived as just what they are: legitimate students with sound academic goals and also serious athletes who participate for much the same reasons as male athletes. Female participation in sports and athletics has become the subject of extensive commentary, and good studies are included in the definitive works cited earlier by Weiss and Novak (*Sport: A Philosophic Inquiry; The Joy of Sports*), and also in Michener's *Sports in America* and the anthology by Talamini and Page *Sport and Society*. One of the more significant articles on the subject is Jane English's "Sex Equality in Sports" (1978).[11]

Faculty Attitudes: Bias and Prejudice

Probably the most sensitive area of the college experience for intercollegiate student-athletes involves the bias and prejudice they really encounter or at least perceive in some faculty members in their academic relationship. This bias and prejudice extend in both directions—some faculty members are perceptually prejudiced in favor of athletes and tend to be sympathetic in the relationship, while other faculty members are perceptually prejudiced against athletes and tend to be intolerant in academic procedures. Bias and prejudice were mentioned earlier as ubiquitous deficiencies in the human spirit, and probably nothing much more can be added in the context of faculty attitudes. It should be observed that alleged faculty bias and prejudice extend beyond athletics into such areas as race and sex and major academic fields: "I don't want any athletes in my classes, and I don't want any minority groups or females either....Those pre-med majors don't want to learn—all they worry about is A grades so they can get into med school....Those business administration people have their heads in a ledger and can't relate to anything cultural or ideological."

One tends to hear facile and pseudo-psychological assessments of some faculty members as frustrated and/or disillusioned former athletes, along with references to the popular image of college professors as ascetic and intellectual elites with little or no feel for physical existence. Some interesting national studies indicate a curious ambivalence in the image of faculty members in American colleges and universities. These studies are cited in an article by Robert T. Blackburn and Michael S. Nyikos "College Football and Mr. Chips: All in the Family" (October 1974).[12] The studies indicate that individually faculty members are much more athletically inclined than the popular image would suggest, and rank high in the percentage of amateur participants (notably in running and racquet games) and are faithful if sometimes furtive spectators at intercollegiate athletic contests. The studies add that the more prestigious the institution usually the higher the percentage of individual faculty participation and spectatorship. "At intellectually elite and bucolic Carleton, over 80% of the faculty attend athletic contests and over 60% personally participate in some sport."

> The fictional image of the professor as an effete recluse who lies down at the mere thought of exercise until the idea passes, and who would never be caught dead at an athletic event, is simply a gross distortion of reality. A very large number of faculty people really like sports....competitive behavior is consistent with faculty values and not contradictory. Faculty set high standards for themselves as well as for others. They admire the self-discipline and self-sacrifice a quality performance demands.... professors respect expertise—in the scholar, the string quartet, and the smoothly functioning backfield.[13]

The studies indicate that the ambivalence in faculty attitudes about sports and athletics originates in the collective image projected by faculty members as a group. Collectively faculty members tend to project an aloof, arrogant, and disdainful attitude toward intercollegiate and professional sports, and only grudgingly accept college athletic programs as necessary evils. Their professional mandate is to extol and exalt scholarship and rationality as the highest academic values, and this conflicts with their private acceptance and support of sports and athletics. "Mr. Chips behaves differently when speaking for himself than he does when on the floor of the faculty senate." Their collective defense usually utilizes three standard ploys which can be summarized as follows: Freudian repression of the whole issue by preventing or aborting debates on the legitimacy of intercollegiate athletics; adoption and support of proposals and platforms which are academically correct but have no real bearing or impact on the structure or the future of intercollegiate athletics; and suggesting reforms rather than the abolition of intercollegiate athletics.

> They elect a distinguished and able and revered colleague and instruct him to institute reforms that will bring back the good old days when all that really mattered was how you played the game and not who won. Even if all the other members of the conference are evil and only acting to ensure a victorious team for themselves, we wish to be pure....And so the individual and collective faculty guilt is transferred to one saintly individual and the whole ugly business is buried for another year.[14]

Intercollegiate student-athletes who express their opinions on the issue privately and publicly feel rather strongly that they are sometimes discriminated against by some faculty simply because they are athletes. Their perception is that they are hurt more than they are helped by being student-athletes. The star performers in major sports at a given school are readily recognized by almost all faculty members because of their local and national publicity, and therefore tend to bear the brunt of the burden. Most, if not all, athletes in a given institution eventually come to be recognized or identified through various procedures and thus come to be vulnerable to the process. Many colleges and universities use some system of academic evaluation forms for student-athletes sent periodically to their professors, and such a system quickly identifies student-athletes in given groups and throughout the school. These systems are meritorious in themselves and with proper cooperation are generally beneficial to the student-athletes and to faculty members themselves. Faculty members are also frequently notified by the institution's athletic department regarding necessary absences by student-athletes for traveling purposes and contests and practice sessions. One of the paradoxical results from all this is student-athletes' complaints that they are monitored too much and too closely compared to nonathlete students. Incidentally, students in some of the other special student categories mentioned earlier (underprivileged students, honors students) sometimes complain about similar perceived discrimination related to special identification processes.

Probably the fundamental type of complaint by intercollegiate student-athletes in this area is their perception that some faculty members tend to write-off student-athletes as non-serious students before they have a chance to prove themselves. Many student-athletes feel that some faculty members have preconceived suspicions about the intellectual ability and academic ambition of athletes and are reluctant to accept student-athletes on a par with other students. Typical comments stemming from this view often center on the perception of a double standard allegedly used by some faculty members regarding make-up examinations, submission of late classroom assignments and absences from class. Student-athletes who talk about this say such things as "...I know that if I wasn't an athlete he would have let me take the make-up exam—he let other people in the class take it...she let other people turn in that paper late but she wouldn't take mine...I told him we had an away game and I gave him my cut-slip but he said he didn't care—and half the people in that class are absent half the time anyway." Some faculty members in turn contend that student-athletes take advantage of the situation and sometimes abuse whatever privileges they deserve. Probably this happens on occasion and any such tendencies must be deplored, but nonathlete students sometimes take unfair advantage of extracurricular involvements and responsibilities in much the same manner.

In the interests of balance and justice, it must be emphasized that such comments and contentions reflect *perceptions* by intercollegiate student-athletes with no attempt at empirical justification or statistical foundation. Much of this may be simply parroted or handed down from one generation of student-athletes to the next with no real attempt at objective evaluation, and some of it may be said just to fit the popular image of things. Statistics are well-nigh impossible since faculty members are understandably reluctant to shout their prejudices for or against athletes for all the world to hear. The consolation and the balance occur in the unanimous contention by intercollegiate student-athletes that the vast majority of faculty members are fair and objective in their academic relationship with student-athletes and nonathlete students alike. This relates to the contention that intercollegiate athletics and the activities of many student-athletes contribute measureably to the image of the institution for better or for worse, and this must be understood in the acceptance and treatment of student-athletes.

Mandates for Institutions

It can be maintained that the cardinal sin for colleges and universities is the exploitation of students for athletic purposes unrelated to the fundamental institutional mandate to *educate* and to develop the intellectual potential and cultural sophistication of all students. The sometimes subtle but de facto denial of meaningful college education for some students at some institutions in the name of athletic achievement is particularly distasteful because it involves the scarring of such lofty ideals and such sacred trusts. Academically honest colleges and universities with nationally competitive sports programs must observe the basic guideline that intercollegiate student-athletes are students first and athletes second in the context of their college experience. Such institutions must establish some system of empirical evidence to monitor student-athletes' academic progress and ensure their timely graduation, and the measuring devices should be rigorous, extensive, and effective.

Colleges and universities with serious sports programs must be reasonably and justly concerned about the unique physical and psychological pressures and unusual time-energy demands on student-athletes, and must recognize the reciprocal and mutually beneficial character of the institution's contractural agreement with student-athletes. Such institutions are morally obligated to provide the climate and the motivational support for successful academic performance and balanced athletic achievement with integrity and probity for the institution and for the serious student-athlete. Sports and athletics are an integral and indispensable aspect of higher education in contemporary society, and intelligent and humanistic concern for the academic success of intercollegiate student-athletes can only enhance the stature and prestige of our colleges and universities and contribute to the pursuit of human excellence.

CHAPTER SIX

Collegiate Athletic Programs: Techniques for Integrity

P roceeding from the principles and conclusions established in the preceding discussion of intercollegiate sports and athletics, this chapter focuses on the instruments, techniques, and attitudes necessary to guarantee meaningful academic progress and timely graduation for intercollegiate student-athletes. The noblest educational ideals and the best theoretical intentions by academic administrators are futile and unavailing without systems of practical application and consistent measurement of performances and goals. It is imperative that colleges and universities have empirical evidence indicating constructive concern about the fundamental issues relating to student-athletes delineated in the previous chapter: recognition and emphasis on the orientation of student-athletes as students first and athletes second; reasonable and just recognition of the unique physical and psychological pressures and unusual time-energy demands on student-athletes; recognition of the mutually beneficial character of the institution's contractural agreement with student-athletes; and willingness to restrict privileges and considerations for student-athletes to NCAA and AIAW recommendations and regulations (and to what is available in principle to other students).[1]

In much the same way that sports and athletics constitute a microcosm of society and thus reflect the ills of society, intercollegiate sports and athletics are caught up in the problems of contemporary higher education and have become (in John Underwood's graphic phrase) "the spoor of an educational system gone mad." Many of the difficulties in both areas stem from the rapid and immense growth of our higher educational system over the past three decades, resulting in new dimensions and new concepts of academic and financial planning and management. This surge of bigness originates with vastly expanded possibilities and opportunities for college and university matriculation (beginning with the GI Bill following World War

II), and culminates in greatly increased student populations including the establishment of a national network of junior colleges and off-campus branches of parent institutions. Added to this growth factor are the commonly cited allegations about our educational system from the ground up: the apathy of parents who fail to encourage and direct their children's academic progress; the failure of elementary school educators to teach the basics of meaningful learning; the practice of high school administrators and faculty (frequently beset with discipline problems) in moving students as quickly as possible toward graduation rather than education; and the minimal entrance requirements for junior colleges and branch campuses. The growth factor and these inherent flaws are compounded by inflationary costs and expenses in maintaining colleges and universities, and the result is that academic adminstrators are confronted with a tangle of problems requiring new dimensions and new concepts in planning and management. The final straw is the current downward trend in student population accompanied by sharp declines in tuition revenue and new concerns for the economic survival of smaller institutions.

This need to recognize changes and to confront new dimensions is reflected in a recent report issued by the University of Southern California after the institution was sanctioned by the Pacific 10 Conference for academic violations:

> (One of the weaknesses leading to the present crisis) has been failure to comprehend the significance of changes that have occurred in competitive sports in America during the past three decades. Colleges and universities today must come to grips with these changes because they are the source of much of the malaise that afflicts intercollegiate athletics today. The earlier brief crisis of the 50's came at a time when national television played a small part; when pro football and basketball were in a fledgling state, and big-time professional tennis and golf were almost unimaginable; when the largest pro contracts might total $30,000 per year and agents to negotiate them were rare; when the egalitarian 'Great Society' reforms of the 60's, which

broadened higher education's accessibility, had not yet begun; when literacy levels in elementary and secondary schools were not declining; and when Las Vegas-style gambling on collegiate sports was less prominent. Higher education must begin to comprehend the implications of these major developments if it is to begin to deal more adequately with the present crisis.[2]

Collegiate Athletic Programs: The Boon and the Burden

In a curiously paradoxical sense, the unprecedented stature of contemporary intercollegiate sports and athletics is at once a thorn and a rose for contemporary higher education. The subject of this survey and analysis is the plight of intercollegiate athletic programs allegedly plagued with abuses and corruptions, resulting in serious criticism relating to the validity of intercollegiate athletics and the integrity and probity of college presidents, athletic directors, coaches, and players. The other side of the coin is that successful (winning) intercollegiate sports programs are a source of significant revenue from gate receipts and contributions from proud alumni and especially from lucrative television contracts for regular and post-season games. Such revenue eases much pain and justifies the athletic program as an instrument in assuring the academic well-being and future of the college or university. In a crass way of putting such things, college administrators who are assured of large annual incomes from successful sports programs are tempted to refrain from evaluating the philosophies and practices of athletic directors and coaches with proven track records. Even in more modest programs without such income (and many smaller and non-winning programs operate at a loss), intercollegiate sports and athletics are valuable in terms of intangible and incidental returns from loyal students and alumni who live in the hope that the program will become bigger and better.

Certainly the blame for abuses and corruptions in intercollegiate sports and athletics should be distributed, but academic administrators and athletic department personnel who perpetuate the system must be implicated more than student-athletes who may be aware of the situation but powerless to change it without sacrificing their careers. This is reflected in the references already cited and is repeated in significant commentary from a variety of sources. An elite panel of educators and sports figures (including John Wooden, Joe Paterno, and John Underwood) analyzes the issue in the scholarly *Phi Delta Kappan* (September 1980) in the context of "Student-Athletes: Tackling the Problem."[3] The article begins with a quotation from a recent report by the American Council on Higher Education:

> It is the (college) president's responsibility to insure integrity in athletic operations, the ACE said in a policy statement after a three-year study by the organization's Commission on Collegiate Athletics. Some presidents 'have generally ignored' that responsibility, the ACE suggested, thereby letting an ugly situation build: an 'emphasis on the revenues and expenses of athletics rather than on the institution's educational programs and increased (even excessive) pressures to win' in order to pay the program's bills.
>
> The report (is issued) with a warning: 'If key administrators do not get involved, then the inevitable will happen: There will be scandals, government involvement...and public condemnation.[4]

This is reiterated in remarks by John Wooden, one of the most erudite and most humanistically oriented coaches in modern sports history, who says bluntly that "...In my opinion, the ills of intercollegiate athletics come from management. I don't believe the presidents take a strong enough hand to make sure that the program is functioning as it should...."[5] Similar sentiments are expressed by Joe Paterno, an equally sensitive and concerned athletic director and coach:

> My feeling has been for many years that the university presidents and the faculties of many institutions have just walked

down the halls and looked at the ceilings. They didn't want to see anything. They've evaded responsibility and they've compromised themselves in such a way that it's almost impossible at this time to get back into the situation.[6]

California State University (Long Beach) President Stephen Horn, long an advocate of reform in intercollegiate athletics and one of the pioneers among college presidents to attend NCAA national conventions, broadens the scope somewhat in implicating faculty members as well as administrators:

Problems such as forged transcripts and unearned academic credit are obviously not the sole responsibility of coaches. However, we should not naively believe that good old Professor Chips violates institutional integrity out of the kindness of his heart. Often there is a connection between the coaches and many overzealous faculty and community 'groupies' who enjoy the prerequisites of attending practice, traveling with the team, and sitting on the bench. Are these zealots seeking a lost youth? I don't know....

I agree that college presidents should play a greater role in straightening out intercollegiate athletics. Some have tried, and as a result some progress has been made. However, too many either do not care or do not want to tangle with the wheeler-dealers whose money in the bank and fat TV contracts seem to drive the intercollegiate athletic machine....[7]

Athletic Involvement and Academic Performance

Despite this justified concern about abuses and corruptions in intercollegiate sports and athletics, it is safe to say that most student-athletes in most of the nine-hundred member institutions in the NCAA (and AIAW) are serious and capable students, and that the institutions themselves are genuinely and properly concerned about their realistic academic progress and timely graduation. Authenticated statistics frequently indicate that student-athletes collectively perform as well and sometimes better compared to nonathlete students. In the typical Eastern college whose policy statements on the importance of sports and athletics are cited in the previous chapter, the pertinent figures for a representative semester are as follows: student-athletes received 19.6 percent A grades compared to 25.5 percent for other students; 36.3 percent B grades to 33.9 percent for other students; 84 percent C grades to 82.1 percent for other students; 3.6 percent failing grades to 4.2 percent for other students; and 3.9 percent course withdrawals to 4.2 percent for other students.[8] The common contention that athletes benefit from being routed to certain instructors and less demanding courses is not necessarily true and will be discussed later in this chapter. Many academically successful student-athletes are convinced that the discipline and motivation of sports and athletics extend into their classroom experiences, and this frequently results in academic achievement unprecedented in their scholastic careers.

It might be speculated that student-athletes should perform better academically in the off-seasons of their respective sports, when theoretically there should be less immediate pressure and a greater sense of freedom and diversion. The fallacy here is that the nature of contemporary intercollegiate athletics makes the old concept of off-seasons a luxury of the past. The scope and intensity of contemporary intercollegiate sports programs lead to the reality of year-round involvement in most major sports in the typical curriculum. Basketball now routinely includes summer leagues which are largely mandatory for progress and exposure, and so-called "informal" practice sessions before and after the regular seasons where attendance and performance are carefully, if covertly, monitored. Football routinely includes spring training designed for intense and productive performance at the individual and team levels, and a year-round mandatory program of weight-training and physical conditioning. Once a spring sport in nature and campus appeal, baseball now begins much earlier in propitious climates and continues as long as there is reason to hold college students together, and in less favorable climates the concept of fall baseball has taken hold. Sports such as track and field and swimming routinely extend through the fall, winter, and spring; and this attitude of total commitment is reflected in other sports in various ways. The situation of female student-athletes is comparable in that most female student-athletes are multi-sport performers, and often their athletic grant-in-aid is based upon participation in basketball, field hockey, and softball (among other combinations).

One of the critical statistics in this general context is the graduation rate for student-athletes compared to nonathlete students. This is mentioned frequently in descriptions of academic/athletic irregularities, both in terms of low graduation rates for student-athletes and false and manipulated graduation rates (usually by neglecting to include student-athlete dropouts). Studies in this area indicate a reported national average graduation rate of about 50 percent for athletically oriented institutions (major sports programs), and the University of New Mexico was cited as a negative example in the 1979 scandals with an alleged student-athlete graduation rate of 21 percent.[9] When graduation rates for athletes are legitimately low, the institution obviously should re-evaluate the nature of its concern and commitment regarding the academic well-being and progress of its student-athletes.

Some critics of the intercollegiate scene stress that many student-athletes exceed the normal four-year period for matriculation and graduation, but this is relatively insignificant so long as it is kept within reason. Extended college experiences and careers are by no means limited to student-athletes, since statistics indicate that only 65 percent of typical student populations graduate in the prescribed four-year period. Many students extend their college years for travel or work experience and other ways of "finding themselves." The NCAA sanctions the five-year plan for graduation but restricts athletic eligibility to four years of varsity competition.

Probably the most significant criterion of academic authenticity for student-athletes (and other students) is the proper understanding and enactment of the concept of "normal progress toward an academic degree and graduation." The traditional interpretation originally mandated by the NCAA is a 2.0 grade-point average (on a scale of 4.0) which usually translates into a "C" standard. Although the NCAA now leaves the interpretation of "normal degree progress" to the discretion of individual institutions, many colleges and universities utilize the 2.0 rule for athletic eligibility (and eligibility for other extracurricular activities). The weakness and exploitation aspect of the 2.0 GPA is that it is relatively easy for any student to maintain such an average (if this is the only objective) by taking courses randomly and applying some systematic version of the course withdrawal process. This approach is even easier in institutions with curricula designed specially for student-athletes: the proverbial "Basket-weaving I and II" courses and "Essentials of Basketball Theory" or "Basic Components of the J-Stroke."

Assuming that none such courses are included in the curriculum and student-athletes are required to take the same courses and follow the same degree programs as nonathlete students, the proper interpretation of academic progress and degree completion is based on the number and sequence of required courses in standard academic tracks leading to specific academic degrees. This is readily measurable semester by semester and year by year, and student-athletes (and all students) should be aware personally and through administrative dictum of their systematic progress. This awareness should be monitored by the academic administrator for the athletic program and faculty advisors, and the process should never be relegated to assistant coaches or other athletic department personnel. Instances of failure to maintain the prescribed academic schedule should be communicated and corrected through the proper channels.[10]

Even the most academically sincere colleges and universities with nationally competitive sports and athletic programs run the risk periodically of some highly publicized cases of student-athlete academic neglect and failure. This is the nature of things and points up incidentally another notable difference in the life and times of student-athletes compared to nonathlete students. Many nonathlete students are also periodically guilty of academic neglect and failure, but their cases are rarely held up for the world to see and for the institution to endure. Student-athletes who incur academic probation for low grades could suffer much more privately and publicly compared to nonathlete students in the same situation. Student-athletes on academic probation are vulnerable technically at least to losing their athletic grant-in-aid, since such grants are contingent upon satisfactory academic progress among other things.

In institutions which publish probation lists at the end of the traditional fall semester, student-athletes in some sports (notably basketball) could have their careers interrupted in mid-season, and such cases usually become public knowledge with damaging effects for the athlete's personal and academic reputation. The NCAA leaves discretion about the timing of probation reports to individual institutions, and some schools report probations only at the end of the academic year rather than after each semester. In contrast to all this, nonathlete students on academic probation generally have much less to lose in terms of their private lives and public notoriety.

Techniques for Integrity

In colleges and universities with intelligent and constructive concern about student-athletes' academic progress and timely graduation, the basic mechanism for benevolent control is usually some form of systematic counseling and tutoring tailored for the student-athlete program. It is essential that this counseling and guidance be administered by professional academicians rather than athletic department personnel—or even athletic department personnel under the guidance of faculty administrators. Student-athletes are normally inducted into these special aid programs immediately upon matriculation, and sometimes in the late summer weeks preceding their freshman year. They should receive counseling and advice on rostering and course selection and other aspects of placement in prescribed educational tracks, including follow-up procedures and systematic performance measurements. Many student-athletes do not necessarily need the program, and some even resent this constructive control of their academic affairs: some perceive this as a form of discrimination in that they are monitored too much and too closely compared to nonathlete students.

Campus critics and sometimes the general public tend to misinterpret this special attention for student-athletes in two respects. The first is the notion that such counseling favors student-athletes with singular privileges compared to nonathlete students, and the second is the contention that student-athletes in the program are deliberately routed to selected sympathetic faculty members and notoriously easy courses of study. The first notion is fallacious since every academically progressive college and university provides similar counseling for *all* students and not just student-athletes. All incoming students are expressly and publicly advised of various special counseling opportunities, and such information is available in a variety of ways throughout their college experience.

The second contention that such programs are designed to place student-athletes with certain professors and/or in certain courses is ill-conceived, since the purpose of counseling directors with personal and professional integrity is just the opposite: to guarantee that student-athletes will roster for required courses and programs rather than taking courses randomly. Student-athletes who are so inclined learn about easy professors and easy courses in the same way that all students learn about such things: by word of mouth through the campus grape-vine in its various manifestations. Student-athletes who follow such peer guidance simply imitate other students who have particular goals or objectives (or none at all). Many students in various major fields attempt to avoid courses which, in their opinion, have no bearing on their real or imagined professional future (math and science for some, literature and philosophy for others), and deliberately register for reputedly easy professors when they are required to take such courses.

It must be emphasized also that opportunities for special counseling and academic guidance are usually even more readily available in specifically designed programs for other special-interest student groups mentioned in the preceding chapter (honors program students, educationally and socially deprived students, military veteran students). Such student categories generally have the benefit of unique opportunities in registering courses and selection of major field requirements and other academic procedures. Special counseling programs for student-athletes are neither more nor less discriminatory than similar programs for other selected segments of the student population.

In the final analysis, it is in the interests of common sense and justice that colleges and universities with ethically oriented sports and athletic programs should have designated counseling and guidance systems for student-athletes. The institution presumably has extensive financial investments in the athletic program itself and in student-athlete support systems, and certainly has moral obligations relating to the mutually beneficial character of the agreement between student-athletes and the college or university. It is much to the institution's advantage to have properly oriented and properly directed student-athletes who will succeed academically and thereby continue to serve their own athletic interests and the interests of the school.

Institutional Responsibility: Policies and Procedures

In the administrative structure of typical colleges and universities, the campus offices most directly and most frequently involved with the routine implementation of student policies (including athletic policy) are: 1) the admissions office; 2) the registrar's office (or the office responsible for grade reports and transcripts); and 3) the office of student affairs, including the area of student discipline. These offices embody the image and character of the institution, and usually provide empirical measurements relating to goals and purposes and outcomes. These are critical offices with respect to institutional policy for the student population in general, and especially for special student categories including student-athletes. This is clearly reflected in the consistent implication of these offices in reports of academic/athletic irregularities and abuses.

ADMISSIONS OFFICES

Admissions offices in colleges and universities must be acutely aware of the importance of constructive admissions policies for the present and the future of the institution, including the nature and function of selective or flexible admissions policies for special student categories. The basic principle of intelligent admissions policy is to admit routinely qualified students who will benefit from the college experience and who will benefit the institution tangibly or intangibly, and to admit certain marginal students in special student categories for the mutual benefit of the student and the institution. These academically marginal students frequently offer unusual skills or abilities at least tangentially related to the educational process, which can be utilized for the betterment of the institution—including sports and athletics. Assuming that such marginal students have a least minimal entrance credentials (including the projected 2.0 GPA if applicable), constructive admissions policy would be to decide on the basis of two considerations: can the student succeed on his or her own merits; and can the student succeed with the systematic counseling and guidance offered in every academically sincere college or university.

With respect to student-athletes, admissions policies are

consistent in institutions with nationally competitive sports programs. Where there is a problem with marginal academic credentials for gifted student-athletes, colleges and universities with nationally competitive athletic programs (including some of the most academically prestigious schools in the nation) have flexible admissions standards and to think otherwise is naive. As indicated in so many ways in this book, intercollegiate sports and athletics constitute an important and integral part of higher education and in some institutions guarantee financial solvency, and blue-chip athletic prospects are worth the interpretation of standard institutional policies and procedures. One rubric many institutions utilize in this context is to designate a certain percentage of admissions cases as "open admissions" with no standards required (or at least not the usual standards for other admissions), and student-athletes are often admitted on such a basis. Athletic coaches often "strongly recommend" admission for gifted student-athletes with and without attractive entrance credentials, and responsible admissions offices must resist such pressure from athletic department personnel. It must be the admissions office which admits all the students and not the coaches or the athletic director or sympathetic campus agencies. Part of the irony in the situation is that coaches understandably feel a sense of chagrin when highly regarded athletic prospects are denied admission to their school, and then enroll in competitive institutions with different admissions standards.

Again it must be emphasized that admissions policies for student-athletes (along with other student policies) must be evaluated in the context of admissions policies for other special-interest student categories mentioned frequently in this discussion. Applicants for admission to special programs for educationally deprived students and older students and continuing education students and others all have the benefit of flexible admissions standards, and in many institutions military veterans and faculty dependent students are admitted on an open admissions basis. The flexibility potential for admitting some marginal students is really quite diverse, and usually reduces to the principle implicit in the student-athlete program: the possibility of a mutually beneficial relationship for the student and for the institution. Most colleges and universities admit some marginal students whose academic potential can be developed for their personal benefit, and who have talents and abilities to make the institution somehow better for their presence.

REGISTRAR'S OFFICES

One of the most sensitive offices in any college or university is the office responsible for the submission of grades and student records and the preparation of transcripts—duties normally associated with the registrar's office. This office is intimately involved in one of the most critical areas of the college experience for all students including student-athletes. The recording of grades and the preparation of transcripts constitute the most visible and probably the most meaningful expression of the educational process, and the honesty and integrity of these procedures reflect the honesty and integrity of the institution itself. Most of the institutional scandals relating to athletics focus on the forgery and manipulation of grades and transcripts between schools and within individual institutions, including grades and academic credits awarded for mythical courses non-held in empty garages hundreds of miles from the recording college or university.

Registrar's offices in self-respecting colleges and universities must resist any direct or indirect pressures from athletic department personnel for altering or falsifying grades and transcripts, and there should be no provisions in student-athlete academic policy permitting interpretation of standard recording procedures. Here again in the context of registrar's office relationships with student-athletes, the situation must be extended to include other special student categories on campus. Many institutions have interpretative or different recording procedures for programs involving educationally deprived students and continuing education students and others. An example is to permit students in such programs to have letter grades (A-B-C-D-F) changed to the usually more lenient "pass-fail" option—sometimes months after the original grade is submitted. There is no necessary suggestion of impropriety in such procedures but they are *different* compared to the rest of the student population, and in this respect student-athletes might be denied privileges extended to other special student groups.

In addition to the processing of grades and transcripts, another routine function normally administered by the registrar's office is the business of registering students for specific courses and classes. Campus critics sometimes contend that student-athletes receive preferred treatment in this area, and this may be true, but there are logically compelling reasons. In many intercollegiate sports and athletic programs, the normal time period for practice sessions and contests in some sports is the late afternoon hours—theroretically after the close of the school day. Athletic directors and coaches and student-athletes prefer and request earlier class schedules to avoid unnecessary conflicts with practices and games. This is more of a problem for some student-athletes than for others depending on the sport and the season and the availability of (lighted and indoor) campus facilities. Most football and basketball programs traditionally have practice sessions in the late afternoon, and most baseball and soccer and field hockey teams practice and frequently play scheduled contests in this time period. In the context of the institution's commitment to an athletic program, it seems only reasonable that such relatively minor rostering adjustments should be made for these athletic obligations. And where it is feasible and applicable, the same considerations should be extended to nonathlete students engaged in significant school-related extracurricular activities.

CAMPUS DISCIPLINARY OFFICES

Besides the admissions office and the registrar's office, another critical institutional office is the administrator for student life and student affairs, including the area of student discipline and disciplinary procedures. Student-athletes tend to be particularly involved with this office—primarily because athletes usually comprise the largest designated group of on campus residents, and are usually the most permanent residents (during holiday periods and "off-season" periods for the rest of the student population). In the context of special privileges and considerations for student-athletes in this area, opinion varies as to whether athletes should be housed together as a distinct community in specific campus dwellings, or whether they should be dispersed and mingled with nonathlete students in buildings open to all. Some colleges and universities with major sports programs have notoriously lavish complexes for athletes in certain sports (the Paul W. Bryant Hall at the University of Alabama is frequently mentioned), while in other institutions the accommodations are more modest but still reserved for student-athletes only.

Commonly cited advantages in having student-athletes in given sports live together focus on opportunities for establishing and solidifying team unity and a sense of "togetherness," and also the convenience of academic/athletic administrative communication with the players. Advantages of having student-athletes live with other students emphasize opportunities for social, cultural, and intellectual growth and diversification, and a greater sense of meaningful involvement in the larger educational community represented in the school. In colleges and universities where living accommodations for student-athletes are markedly different and superior compared to housing for other students, there is likely to be some understandable resentment among other components of the larger college community and a greater sense of divisiveness and suspicion regarding student-athletes. Reasonable special privileges accorded student-athletes would include immediate availability of campus housing (the NCAA mandates that athletes on full grants must be guaranteed housing), and preferential location in dorms located near athletic complexes for everyone's convenience. Some minor special living accoutrements are also in order, such as the availability of seven-foot beds for some members of some basketball teams.

Campus disciplinary attitudes and procedures frequently serve as a barometer of student life in the context of responsible adaptation to the academic environment. Here again student-athletes frequently suffer more privately and publicly compared to nonathlete students. Instances of student-athlete infractions of campus codes are usually highly publicized in the media, and dismissals result of course in the loss of athletic grants-in-aid. Nonathlete students who commit the same infractions have their privacy protected and usually have less to lose personally in connection with dismissal from school. In the normal course of things, many academic disciplinarians feel that well-motivated student-athletes tend to be a constructive influence on campus and make positive contributions to the image and well-being of the institution.

Academics and Athletics: Meeting the Twain

In terms of sanity and perspective in intercollegiate athletics and the academic careers of student-athletes, the most important recommendation is that colleges and universities must consistently regard student-athletes as students first and athletes second. This regard must be expressed in intelligent concern for student-athletes' realistic academic progress and graduation and career planning. Probably not enough has been said specifically about the importance of career planning beyond graduation for student-athletes. Given the nature of intercollegiate sports and athletic involvement, there is the tendency even among well-meaning educators and well-motivated student-athletes to think (to idealize) about continued athletic participation after graduation. But statistics and reality indicate that a miniscule proportion of college athletes ever play professionally in any sport, and an equally small number continue to be involved in coaching and athletic administration. When the dream dies it is important that constructive career planning can fill the void and guarantee a meaningful future.

This fundamental need to recognize student-athletes as students first and athletes second is generally accepted in academically sincere colleges and universities, but even here the requirement is frequently glossed over and inadequately implemented. The dual characterization as student and athlete requires mutual caring and shared responsibility that often go unrecognized in the routine life of colleges and universities. Since student-athletes are both students and athletes, it is imperative that both academicians and athletic department personnel should care and share responsibility together for the well-being and progress of student-athletes. In the daily life of many colleges and universities, this mutuality of interest is often neglected and the components exist like twain that shall never meet.

Usually there isn't nearly enough personal recognition and personal interchange between academic administrators and faculty members and their opposite numbers in the athletic administration. There is often the danger, if not the reality, of a destructive dichotomy on campus separating these two main influences in the life of student-athletes. Both components must develop mutual acceptance and respect and trust, and must become visible and accessible to each other as individuals and as members of the college community. Too many administrators and faculty members have no real consciousness of the individuals in the sports complexes, and too many athletic directors and coaches have no real consciousness of the individuals in the halls of learning. What is needed in many schools is a concerted public relations program extending in both directions from *academe* to athletics designed to guarantee mutual recognition and visibility and acceptance. Academic administrators and faculty members are probably limited with respect to practical occasions for such interchange (apart from attendance at contests and practices), but a viable medium would be regular attendance by athletic department personnel at academic receptions and convocations and faculty meetings including senate meetings. Every effort should be made to establish a combined faculty of educators in the arts and in athletics.

This philosophy of interaction must be implemented through systems and instruments involving academic administrators and special counselors and eventually athletic directors and coaches. Usually the basic mechanism for this practical implementation is some form of the specially designed counseling and guidance programs for student-athletes discussed previously. In addition to providing initial academic advice and orientation, an important function of such programs is the systematic collection and evaluation of pertinent information relating to student-athletes' academic performance and progress. This is usually accomplished through the use of printed evaluation forms sent periodically to faculty members to report the academic status of student-athletes registered for their courses. These forms are returned to the administrators of the counseling program, who incorporate the information into a standing statistical study of each athlete's status as the basis for any remedial procedures. Faculty members thus become the strongest (or the weakest) link in the system, and the practical value of the entire procedure depends on the conscientious cooperation of professors in returning these forms promptly and with sufficient detail for evaluation and guidance. The forms themselves should be concise and easy to complete to encourage cooperation, and pertinent academic administrators should instruct faculty members to cooperate for the mutual benefit of student-athletes and the institution.

The information gathered and evaluated in the counseling and guidance system is eventually communicated to the academic advisor for student-athletes (who should be an integral member of the program itself), and then to athletic directors and coaches. While the counseling and guidance program must be academically based and administered, athletic department personnel and especially coaches must be involved in the system. It is the responsibility of coaches especially to know the academic status of their athletes, and to encourage academic effort and cooperation in attending classes, completing examinations, and performing in a conscientious and dedicated manner. For all the people and factors in the counseling and guidance program, usually the closest one-on-one relationship is between coaches and players and this tends to result in the most authoritarian and most effective influence. Coaches naturally have this interest and responsibility (or should have) with respect to their players, and players in turn are more apt to respond more completely to their coaches with whom they share their athletic careers and aspirations than to academic personnel.

ACADEMIC ATHLETIC ADVISORS

While every person and every function is important in this systematic effort to guarantee realistic academic progress for student-athletes, the key component is an efficient, dedicated, and respected academic advisor for athletics. This should be an administrator or faculty member with significant academic stature on campus, with access and acceptability in all pertinent areas of academic and athletic administration and practice. The responsibility should never be relegated to assistant athletic directors or coaches or any athletic department personnel either on a full-time basis or as "something else for them to do." Academic advisement is an academic matter and requires the educational expertise and motivational concepts associated with professional academicians, who are at once removed from the inner sanctum of the athletic department and yet sympathetic and constructively concerned about realistic academic progress and timely graduation for student-athletes. The self-study report by the University of Southern California cited earlier recognizes this in contending that:

> All matters of eligibility and academic progress must be under the direct supervision and control of faculty and staff outside the department of athletics....

Programs for the advisement and counseling of athletes should be fully integrated with on-going programs within the University's total academic support plan.[11]

Along with the importance and critical role of academic administrators, faculty, and coaches in directing the student-athlete program, it must be emphasized that the primary responsibility for academic success lies with the student-athlete himself or herself. Academic control and direction of the student-athlete program is simply the context for the student-athlete's personal desire and dedication to educational success. The most intelligently designed and most efficiently functioning system is useless and sterile without the individual student-athlete's personal commitment and sincere motivation for higher education. Whatever help the counseling and guidance system provides must begin with self-help. The USC report summarizes this in asserting that:

> The dominant rationale for enrolling in any academic program should be a student's educational needs and priorities. Academic programs should never be manipulated for other ends.
>
> The student-athlete should take an active part in initiating, planning and implementing his or her academic program.
>
> Student-athletes experiencing academic difficulty should accept responsibility for seeking out available academic support services as needed.
>
> The student-athlete must accept responsibility for participation in scheduled learning activities and in the preparation and completion of assignments.[12]

When priorities are properly recognized and properly ordered, sports and athletics and the pursuit of education are eminently compatible and the combination is a significant force in the achievement of human excellence.

CHAPTER SEVEN

Theories
of
Winning

I t is commonly maintained in a variety of forums that the abuses and corruptions in the sporting enterprise (and especially in intercollegiate sports and athletics) are caused by serious over-emphasis on the importance of *winning* above all else. One of the most frequently quoted and most castigated slogans in this context is the phrase commonly attributed to Vince Lombardi but reportedly originated by Jim Tatum at the University of Maryland: "Winning isn't everything—it's the only thing." Despite the critical commentary by well-intentioned sports moralists who turn this to their own advantage, the Lombardi-Tatum contention is fundamentally true—so long as it is properly understood and properly interpreted. This chapter isolates and analyzes the controversial issues of competition and competitiveness and the pursuit of victory, again with special reference to intercollegiate sports and athletics where the distinctions and the subtleties are most often blurred and misinterpreted. The thesis will be that winning with honor and decency is the essence of sports and athletics and the essence of life itself. People who say that winning is not important are superficial and/or preparing for failure in sports and athletics or whatever the activity might be. People who say that winning is more important than decency and honor and integrity are a disgrace to sports and athletics and a disgrace to the human race.

The basic premise is that a sound and successful sports and athletic program designed to cultivate and produce human excellence must be a *winning* program. This is because an important dimension in human excellence in any form is some demonstrable measure of superiority, usually expressed in victorious achievement over whatever opponents or obstacles the situation involves. This can be extended beyond sports and athletics into every form of serious human endeavor where hearts and minds and wills compete for scarce and elusive prizes. It has been contended that "...Victory is the natural estate of every self-respecting person, and no self-respecting person voluntarily accepts defeat." To which it must be added that victory without decency is an empty mockery. And it is certainly true that there are forms of winning apart from the numbers on real and figurative scoreboards. The expenditure of maximum effort along with devotion and dedication to goals and purposes creates winners—no matter what the score or who is listed as the winner or the loser. "To run the good race and to fight the good fight" is an ideal of human perfection and richly deserves the highest private and public rewards.

Some of the controversial character of assertions about the importance of winning stems from counter-arguments contending that competition itself or competing well (without winning) is sufficient to guarantee human excellence, and this view will be examined in detail later. More popular controversy about the importance of winning involves the ethical and moral aspects of sports and athletics and human existence in general. As indicated earlier (see chapter I), there is evidence in various forms that some groups and some individuals in intercollegiate and professional sports have grossly misinterpreted the importance of winning, and read this to mean that victory should be pursued at any and every cost to human decency and integrity. Obviously this must be deplored and sports and athletics must abide by the rules of life and the rules of the game. Unless this is stringently observed in every activity, the excellence is never true excellence and the victory is a sham. It is incongruous and contradictory to suggest that true human excellence in any form should emerge from unethical, immoral, and dehumanizing practices. The virtues and values of the sporting enterprise at every level depend on carefully distinguishing between the *business* of winning and the human *art* of physical and spiritual triumph with integrity and probity for participants and for the game itself.

Again this blight on the contemporary sports world must

be recognized and evaluated in the larger context of contemporary society in America and throughout the world. It is empirically evident in routine media coverage of current events that we live in an age of ethical and moral crisis. Probably never before in history has mankind been so aware and so conscious of the need for ethical and moral values; and paradoxically, probably never before has there been such diverse and contradictory interpretations and applications of ethical and moral principles and rules. This is apparent in the highest levels of national and international government and politics, in national and international industry and commerce, and even in some areas of religion and education. As already suggested (see chapter I), the sporting enterprise is a microcosm of society and tends to reflect the ills of an overly mercenary and commercially oriented social structure. This view contends that the malpractices of sports and athletics are symptomatic of spiritual and idealistic deficiencies in our society and culture, and will be corrected only with a reorientation of social values and ideals. The poetic adage that "no man is an island" applies as well to segments of society, and we all benefit, prosper, or decline and fall together. The salvation of society is the salvation of sports and athletics and it behooves us to get on with it for the sake of both components.

It's How You Play the Game

In the wake of increasingly numerous and widely publicized allegations of unethical and immoral practices in the name of *winning* in sports and athletics, many commentators have prescribed a return to "competition for its own sake" to replace emphasis on winning as "the only thing." These are modern prophets of the hallowed adage that "It matters not whether you win or lose, but how you play the game." This at least implies and probably advocates a separation or a distinction between competing with a desire to win and simply competing for its own sake as the measure of excellence. This is a controversial issue both historically and in its current expression, and erudite minds of the past and present have championed these respective views. In many respects the issue deals with the fundamental nature and purpose of sports and athletics beginning with the interpretations and formulations of the ancient Greeks in their classic interest in the sporting enterprise. In their own sophisticated way, the Greeks contended that winning "is the only thing" and heralded the champions who won the prize and wore the coveted laurel wreath. The Greek mind was impervious to second and third-place finishes and to the concept of competing simply for the experience.

The Greek influence tended to prevail for many centuries, and it was not until the nineteenth-century British ideal of games as social institutions—the halcyon era of Matthew Arnold's Rugby College and *Tom Brown's Schooldays*—that the learning lesson of "how you play the game (of life)" took precedence over winning and losing. In a much-respected cultural commentary on the age, John Henry Cardinal Newman's *The Idea of A University* relates to the issue in defining liberal education as that which is self-contained and self-subsistent: "which stands on its own pretensions, which is independent of sequel (and) expects no complement." Education and knowledge in this view reduce to the pursuit itself and the pursuit is everything "without the expectation of sequel and with no end except the enactment of the pursuit itself." Relating this to the world of sports and athletics, it might be maintained that athletic contests are self-contained "learning experiences" which should involve no concern or expectation for the results or "the sequel of winning or losing." The purpose of sports and athletics in this view reduces to the value of the competition itself apart from the values of winning and losing.

Commonly suggested procedural mechanisms for minimizing over-emphasis on winning most frequently center on two aspects of the intercollegiate sports scene (and analogously in all areas of sports and athletics): 1) the introduction of moderate to drastic restrictions on recruiting policies and practices to induce gifted student-athletes to attend given institutions; and 2) the elimination or at least de-emphasis on post-season championship competition at local and national levels. For all the good intentions of their originators, such recommendations contribute little beyond a spiritual prodding to the resolution of whether a sound and successful sports program must be a winning program or merely a competitive program. The problem is that such recommendations beg the usual questions in offering solutions suited perhaps to the ideals but not to the givens—and some of the givens cannot be changed.[1]

Indiscriminate attempts to eliminate recruiting and post-season competition are unwise and even improper for at least two divergent reasons. The first is that such innovations would undermine legitimate attempts to build winning programs with honor and decency and integrity, and would thus contravene the spirit and character of our society and culture. For better or for worse, consistent historical indicators suggest that in our society and in the mainstream of Western civilization *it does matter* whether you win or lose and not just how you play the game. We are the legacy of the Grecian ideal of competing to win the prize, rather than the British ideal of competition for its own sake. Obviously unethical and immoral aspects of sports recruiting and post-season championship competition must be eliminated and avoided at all costs, but our society and culture consistently reflect the Apollonian ideal of meritorious *agon* or worthy struggle and competition to achieve victory. Ironically this is perhaps best indicated in our most academically prestigious colleges and universities: scholars who merely compete without winning significant prizes are not admitted to such institutions, and they do not teach or become administrators at such institutions.

The second reason that ill-conceived attempts to restrict recruiting and post-season play are unwise and improper is more subtle but equally compelling: such developments would unfairly discriminate against student-athletes in intercollegiate programs (and athletes at other levels in the sporting enterprise). As indicated at length in chapter V, student-athletes must be regarded primarily as members of the academic community engaged in the serious pursuit of higher education. Every self-respecting college and university must regard student-athletes as students first and athletes second, and the failure to do so is to renege on the sacred trusts and lofty purposes of *academe*. The problem is that even in the best of circumstances and in the most well-intentioned institutions, very often forms of subtle discrimination come to be directed against student-athletes singled out from the rest of the student population. This tendency toward discrimination was described in previous chapters, and significant aspects are unwittingly implied in gratuitous attempts to de-emphasize basically sound intercollegiate sports and athletic programs.

The best of circumstances and the best of intentions in this area reduce to intercollegiate athletic programs conducted with every respect for ethical and moral precepts wherever they apply, and with serious concern for the academic progress and well-being of student-athletes. Assuming such a situation (and without this assumption nothing constructive can be suggested), any direct or indirect attempts to minimize natural and essential aspects of intercollegiate sports programs are discriminatory to student-athletes, who deserve privileges and considerations consistent with opportunities in other programs in the curriculum. Every college and university in the country sponsors some form of recruitment directed to gifted high school scholars, and many institutions assign administration and faculty members to canvass high schools and to influence potential applicants with acceptable credentials to enroll in the institution. Assuming that the recruitment of gifted student-athletes is equally ethical and legal and in accordance with local and national standards, attempts to minimize or eliminate such recruiting are discriminatory to qualified students who wish to fulfill themselves in sports and athletics rather than history or philosophy or mathematics. Such a policy would be inconsistent with the spirit and intentions of a properly conducted intercollegiate sports program, since such programs should be established in all good faith as legitimate and fully accepted components of the total curriculum with all the privileges and benefits properly pertaining.

The issue of (eliminating) post-season competition in intercollegiate sports and athletics also has parallels in the academic area of the college experience. Liberal knowledge and liberal education at the undergraduate level are never so self-contained nor so self-subsistent that they cannot point beyond this level to more complete fruition and satisfaction in post-graduate education. Academically sincere colleges and universities justifiably encourage gifted undergraduate scholars to seek graduate degrees as an end beyond the basic undergraduate educational experience. While the comparison may be less than exact in every respect, serious participation in intercollegiate sports and athletics points beyond itself to the legitimate opportunity for post-season competition as a means for national recognition and present and future rewards for demonstrated excellence. Again assuming that the forms of post-season competion are constructive and consistent in time and place with academic schedules and requirements, to deny such valid recognition and rewards to student-athletes is to deny these members of the educational community legitimate opportunities for self-fulfillment extended routinely to the rest of the student population.

Always with the understanding that everyone involved must recognize the importance of ethical and moral values whenever they apply, it is reasonable to conclude that competing with a desire to win is naturally compatible with the desire to compete well: there is no need to separate or distinguish the two attitudes—they should go hand in hand and usually they do go hand in hand. To separate the desire to win from the desire to compete well is artificial and il-logical. Athletes and others engaged in serious human pursuits of mind and body who contend that they do not care whether they win or lose are either dilettantes or preparing for failure. In his excellent anthology on *Joy and Sadness in Children's Sports*, Rainer Martens presents an incisive analysis of diverse views on winning and competition in his chapter on "Understanding Competition."[2] Although his remarks are directed primarily to children's participation in sports and athletics, Martens examines the issue in a broader perspective suited to our society and culture. He quotes Gerald Ford's views expressed in a *Sports Illustrated* article (1974) on the importance of winning:

> It has been said...that we are losing our competitive spirit in this country, the thing that made us great, the guts of the free enterprise system. I don't agree with that; the competitive urge is deep-rooted in the American character....We have been asked to swallow a lot of home-cooked psychology in recent years that winning isn't all that important anymore, whether on the athletic field or in any other field, national and international. I don't buy that for a minute. *It is not enough just to compete.* Winning is very important. Maybe more important than ever. (Italics added)[3]

Specifically on the thorny issue of whether children's sports should encourage the spirit of winning or simply competitive participation for its own sake, Martens includes the unequivocal analysis provided by Stephen D. Ward (a practicing psychiatrist and former college athlete and coach) in his "Winning is Everything" essay:

> I am not a believer in the Little League philosophy that everyone who shows up should get to play, regardless of who wins. Athletic contests are the relics and vestiges of what in former times were tribe and life-preserving struggles. I think it is not too far-fetched to parallel our present international political no-win philosophy with our Little League philosophy for juvenile

sports. It is somehow or other not very nice anymore to win. Leo Durocher summed it all up very neatly several years ago when he said 'nice guys finish last.' We are certainly very busy trying to be nice guys....Why delude a child into the belief that success can be achieved by merely presenting himself as an aspiring candidate for the rewards of life? Will his first employer have as gentle a regard as did his Little League manager for the possible psychic trauma that might be done by firing him?

The Little League philosophy fosters security-seeking dependency, acceptance of weakness and goals of mediocrity. It does not breed superior athletes or enterprising citizens.

It has been said that the British Empire was won on the playing fields of Eton. There are many today who would therefore curse those playing fields for having nurtured imperialism and all of its much maligned concomitants. Perhaps too a similar hypothesis could account for the disdain with which intellectuals in general hold athletes and athletics. Perhaps the individual confidence, spirit of enterprise and independence nurtured on our playing fields constitute a threat to our current crop of social, economic, and philosophical planners.

If such be the case, let's get on with the game![4]

It should be observed that Martens' book is designed to present a balanced and objective survey of winning versus competition for its own sake, and corresponding excerpts could be cited about the importance of competition as a value in itself. The sentiments reflected in the preceding remarks obviously support the thesis that winning with decency is the most important aspect of competition in sports and in life itself, and that competition without the desire and the intent to win is a hollow victory. Martens himself offers an insightful summary of the controversy in asserting that:

I find the debate about the value of competition meaningless. Competition is neither good nor bad. It is a social process whereby individuals or groups compare themselves with others using some agreed upon criteria for evaluation. The environment in which a child competes...determines whether the effect of the events encountered during the competitive process is positive or negative. Thus, depending on the circumstances, competition may result in either desirable or undesirable outcomes.

When the consequences are undesirable, the solution *is not* to abolish competition and replace it with cooperative games, as some have advocated. Children need to learn both competitive and cooperative behaviors (and) both competition and cooperation are inherent aspects of sports. The solution is to change the circumstances. The value of competition depends on *how* the competition is conducted, *how* the events are interpreted, and *how* the emphasis is placed on the participation in relation to the outcome. There is nothing wrong with competing—with being intensely competitive, with wanting to win, with striving to best an opponent—so long as one maintains perspective about the relative significance of the participation and the outcome.[5]

Competitiveness and Ability to Win

Much of the debate about the importance of winning with honor versus the importance of competition for its own sake reduces to the proper meaning of competition or *competitiveness*. Even with emphasis on winning as the proper goal of competition, obviously individual athletes and athletic teams sometimes lose matches and games in which they participate. Before establishing and elaborating on this meaning, perhaps some remarks should be made about the "nobility of losing." The substance of this chapter has been concerned primarily and extensively with the importance of winning in sports and athletics as opposed to competition for its own sake, and probably too little has been said about the nature of defeat whenever it happens. Serious athletes and sports teams (and people in general) compete in games and in life against the specter of defeat, and the possibility and reality of losing has its own grace and character and educational function. In certain circumstances and with the right attitude, athletes and people in general can sometimes learn enough from defeat to become better athletes and better persons.

Martens quotes these lines from Edward Walsh's *The New York Times* article "An American Problem: How To Live With Defeat" (1977):

> To fail is to lose face. But ironically, in our lust for victory, we have lost an opportunity to learn valuable lessons taught only by losing. Like death and taxes, failure is a fact of life. Yet we Americans, weaned on winning, dare not stare at the Medusa of defeat, lest we become petrified like the ancient Greeks. Though postprandial orators wax eloquent over the thrill of victory, seldom is heard an encouraging word about learning from the agony of defeat.

> Instead we're fed that line from the Gospel according to Vince Lombardi: 'Winning isn't everything, it's the only thing.' Lombardi never said it that way, but quoted or misquoted, the phrase still sticks like a fishbone in our collective consciousness. In contrast, how many people at sports dinners hear Berton Brayley's 'Prayer of a Sportsman' which says, 'If I should lose, let me stand by the side of the road and cheer the winners as they go by.'[6]

These are noble and valid sentiments, but nevertheless the pendulum eventually swings back to the importance of winning: the agony of defeat is meaningful only in the context of the thrill of victory. Another often-quoted Lombardian statement is that "losing makes the sacrifice harder." Winning is the positive dimension and losing is always measured by the Holy Grail of victory. Serious athletes and people in general who never learn and never experience the joy of victory never really understand the real meaning of defeat. A steady diet of defeat (however excellent the competitive urge) suffocates the human spirit and teaches nothing about the purpose of life and human striving.

Factors in Competitiveness

Returning to the definition of competition or competitiveness in relation to the importance of winning, these concepts themselves are more elusive and more complex than might appear at first glance. Athletes and sports teams that win frequently are not necessarily the most competitive, and in some properly interpreted circumstances even certain patterns of losing can indicate intense competitive ability and the desire to win. Especially in intercollegiate and professional sports and athletic programs (but also throughout the sporting enterprise), competition and the possibility of victory must be evaluated on a multifaceted scale involving several diverse factors. Certainly local, regional, and national championships and won-lost records over a period of time are significant indicators of competitiveness and the ability to win, but these must be conditioned by various considerations including the following:

1. financial superiority of some individual athletes and teams and sports programs either from private enterprise or government funds.

2. relative strength of respective opponents in schedules of games and matches and meets.

3. excessive emphasis on certain sports in professional and intercollegiate sports programs either because of tradition and/or geographical location.

4. special inducements for recruits and retention of individual and team personnel in financial and academic areas and the availability of attractive and superior athletic facilities.

FINANCIAL SUPERIORITY

It is only reasonable to contend that individual athletes and sports programs with greater financial support are better prepared to be competitive and better able to win. Greater financial support usually means the acquisition of better players and coaches (hopefully recruited ethically and morally), and normally means better physical facilities for training and for contests—all resulting in a more constructive and more positive situation in every respect. This is readily apparent in professional sports franchises, and also in colleges and universities with extensive and nationally competitive sports programs financed with literally millions of dollars in athletic funds and budgets. Understandably this has created controversy in some academic circles (and nonacademic circles) over whether such huge sums of money should be spent to support sports and athletics, and one of the justifications is that successful sports programs generate millions of dollars in revenue for their own support and for the general well-being of the institution. The argument is that nationally ranked sports programs (especially football programs) return enough revenue to pay for themselves, and also to finance libraries, laboratories, and professional programs that contribute to the academic potential and enhance the scholarly prestige of the institution.

Certainly greater financial support is no strict guarantee of competitiveness and the ability to win, since such spiritual intangibles as desire, dedication, and sacrifice are equally important and must be present in athletes and coaches and in the orientation of the program. This is perhaps best indicated currently in the realm of professional sports and athletics in connection with the free agency clause in players' contracts (discussed in some detail in previous chapters). This contractual innovation terminates the player's contract under certain conditions and frees the player to sign a more lucrative contract with another team. The availability of gifted talent if the price is right has lured some owners in various franchises to defy the old adage that "you can't buy championships," and attempt to do so with exorbitant salaries and bonuses for desirable players. Specific examples are the New York Yankees in the reign of George Steinbrenner (Reggie Jackson, Catfish Hunter, et al), and the Philadelphia '76ers basketball franchise under Fitz Dixon (George McGinnis, Julius Erving, et al). An intelligent and knowledgeable critique of this approach is offered by Bill Bradley, Princeton basketball All-American and former professional star and now U.S. Senator from New Jersey, in his aptly titled *Sports Illustrated* article "You Can't Buy Heart."

> Wanted: a championship team—now. Will pay any price, test any law, sell any product, join any club, make any promise if it can be assured that champagne will flow over my head as the owner....
>
> During the last 15 years, the nature of ownership in professional basketball has changed from personal to corporate, from the paternalistic to the mechanistic...Nowadays (owners constitute a) new class of entrepreneurs who typically have made their millions in something else—in real estate, rugs, cookies, or fried chicken. They think that basketball is much the same sort of business. The game becomes a product, players become widgets and fans become markets. Occasionally these otherwise good businessmen ignore rudimentary business practices in the pursuit of their new hobby. But more frequently their accustomed methods of evaluation and review prove inadequate in dealing with the diversity of human problems involved in running a professional basketball team....
>
> The owner wants a champion *now*. The general manager (the basketball expert) knows that it takes time and a little luck to assemble the right players. 'You're the genius,' the corporate executive says, 'turn the team around.' The general manager however cannot filter his won-lost record through accounting procedures that will make it seem as if he won more than he lost...But the desire to succeed quickly leads him to go against his better judgment. He suggests, 'let's buy a star.'[7]

And so the star or several stars are bought (sometimes in more ways than one), and the result is usually much different and much less successful than anticipated. Bradley's article emphasizes the importance of *team unity* along with selflessness, dedication, and desire—none of which are essential elements in a purely financial transaction between owners and individual stars of monetary magnitude. "A former pro once summed up what it takes to have a meshed team with the phrase 'You can't buy heart.' That I suppose is what many of us see in a team game and why it is so difficult to achieve."

> You're really betting on the human spirit as much as on mechanical skills. In a day when many workers get paid eight hours' wages for six hours' work, when many politicians ignore the needs of their constituents, and when a lot of policemen fail to show up on a blackout emergency call, why should basketball players be different?[8]

STRENGTH OF SCHEDULES

Competitiveness and the ability to win are naturally reflected in the calibre of opposition chosen or supplied for individual athletes and sports and athletic teams. Good opposition is essential for the production of excellence in every participant, while mediocre or poor opposition renders the entire endeavor largely meaningless. Individual athletes and teams with impressive won-lost records over various versions of the proverbial "Little Sisters of the Poor" haven't proved anything to themselves or to others about the achievement of excellence. By the same kind of measurement, athletes and teams willing to compete against stronger opponents benefit as persons even in a losing cause. Assuming that athletic schedules are properly balanced to assure good opposition and also the possibility of winning at a representative rate, there is no disgrace in losing to some stronger opponents in the schedule—anymore than there is honor in deliberately scheduling and consistently winning over weaker opponents.

EXCESSIVE EMPHASIS ON CERTAIN SPORTS

Competitiveness and the ability to win are conditioned by excessive emphasis on certain sports in some professional and intercollegiate athletic programs, sometimes occasioned by local traditions of unknown origin and sometimes naturally dictated by geographical location—and sometimes a combination of these and other factors. This excessive emphasis usually leads to self-perpetuating dynasties in selected sports, and logically gives such teams and such programs a competitive edge over teams and programs without such emphasis in given sports. Classic examples of the tradition factor are the Green Bay Packers in professional football and Notre Dame and Ohio State in college football, the Boston Celtics in professional basketball and the New York Yankees in professional baseball. On a lesser scale Lehigh University in eastern Pennsylvania has a strong tradition in the sport of wrestling, and Hartwick College in Illinois is a traditional power in soccer. The geographical factor is obvious in the perennial supremacy of intercollegiate baseball and golf and aquatic teams from California, Arizona, Texas, Florida and other southern states. Examples of teams and programs where tradition and geography combine would be the Montreal Canadiens in professional ice hockey, and the University of Southern California in volleyball and water polo.

SPECIAL INDUCEMENTS FOR RECRUITMENT AND RETENTION

Such inducements are normally: 1) financial in character; 2) academically inspired; and/or 3) centered on superior facilities for one or many sports. In whatever form or combination of forms, they usually contribute to greater competitiveness and the ability to win. In professional sports and athletics, such inducements reduce simply to offers of higher salaries and bigger bonuses for players and coaches on the logically plausible theory that such offers result in the acquisition of superior personnel. Thus the richer professional franchises theoretically should be stronger and more successful, although the dangers of attempting to buy success are inherent in the process and were discussed in detail earlier.

The issue of financial inducements exists in intercollegiate sports and athletics as well, and very often figures in alleged violations of NCAA and AIAW regulations and policies. These financial inducements at the intercollegiate level involve athletic grants-in-aid awarded to student-athletes covering the costs of tuition, books, and room and board, and worth in some cases thousands of dollars annually and tens of thousands of dollars over the four-year period of intercollegiate sports participation. The NCAA and AIAW maintain strict regulations and policies governing the nature and the awarding of athletic grants-in-aid, including formal procedures for investigation and punitive legislation in reported instances of alleged violations of the nationally publicized code. Among many other aspects of administrative process, these regulations restrict the number of grants-in-aid permissible in given sports (currently 95 in Division Ia football and 15 in Division I basketball as examples), and provide guidelines for awarding full grants or only partial grants in various sports. Obviously colleges and universities with greater financial resources and ambitious sports programs can offer more grants and more full grants as inducements to recruits, and thus should be more competitive and better able to win.

As might be expected in the nature of things, this area of financial inducements for prospective student-athletes is often implicated in alleged instances of illegal and unethical recruiting cited in NCAA and AIAW monitoring of intercollegiate sports and athletic programs. Valid and authorized athletic grants-in-aid provide for tuition, room and board, books, and some fees (full grants) or a portion of these expenses (partial grants), and no other forms of payment or financial support are permissible under national regulations. NCAA and AIAW investigations and associated media reports have described alleged instances in which recruits were surreptitiously and illegally offered additional financial inducements. These usually translate into cars and apartments, jobs and houses for members of the student-athlete's family, and contrived but well-paying campus employment such as watching for tidal waves in Kansas or verifying that the water in stadium sprinkling systems is sufficiently wet. Colleges and universities with the kind of unconscionable attitudes that would permit such hoaxes without being detected are likely to have a competitive edge in financial inducements to potential recruits, but perhaps it can be maintained that such situations bear within them the seeds of their own corruption.

SUPERIOR FACILITIES

Another special inducement to competitiveness and the ability to win is the availability of attractive and lavishly appointed sports facilities for professional franchises and for given sports or all sports in intercollegiate programs. This factor is frequently associated with the issues of financial superiority and emphasis on certain sports delineated in previous remarks. The availability of superior physical facilities for training and practice and contests normally attracts superior personnel and usually results in more efficient and even more inspired athletic productivity. With the tremendously increased popularity of professional sports over the past several decades, most professional franchises have constructed a variety of aesthetically appealing and functionally excellent practice and playing sites, featuring the most advanced training equipment and plush creature comforts for players, coaches, and fans. Perhaps the most dramatic examples are the domed stadiums in Houston and New Orleans and in a few other cities, and the multimillion dollar sports complexes built along scenic riverfronts in Philadelphia, Cincinnati, St. Louis, and Pittsburgh.[9] An aspect of superior physical facilities is the adoption and utilization of advanced scientific techniques to increase competitiveness and the ability to win, exemplified in the computerized approach to sports success first associated with the Dallas Cowboys and now employed by professional franchises in different sports.

Especially in intercollegiate sports and athletic programs,

the availability of superior facilities is often a strong inducement to gifted student-athletes, with the natural resultant of
stronger, more competitive, and more victorious teams.
Witness the lavish basketball fieldhouses in the Atlantic
Athletic Conference and in Indiana and California (the mystique of Pauley Pavilion), and the hallowed majesty of
Michigan Stadium and the storied field under the Golden
Dome of Notre Dame in college football, and the lush campus
golf courses and Olympic-styled aquatic facilities in southern
and western colleges and universities. Such niceties are
naturally heralded by institutional athletic recruiters to con-
vince blue-chip prospects to attend one school rather than
another, and usually with considerable success since the
facility itself speaks volumes to young athletes fueled by the
dream of major college athletic recognition and achievement.

SUPERIOR ACADEMIC PROGRAMS

In a different vein and with more selective appeal to individual student-athletes, the final special type of inducement
bearing on competitiveness and better teams is the availability of superior academic opportunities and unique
academic programs offered in some colleges and universities.
Some of the more sensitive and more intuitive (and more intelligent) student-athletes deliberately choose institutions
with good sports and athletic programs, and also prestigious
educational credentials in general and in specialized academic
areas. This type of inducement benefits the Ivy League
schools especially in competing with other institutions, and
also colleges and universities with nationally and internationally renowned speciality reputations in medicine, law,
science, and politics. There is little more to be said about this
form of inducement beyond simply stating its existence, but it
is undoubtedly the most authentic and most rewarding reason
for a student-athlete (or any student) to choose a college or
university. This is probably in the realm of ideals, but it
would be a powerful portent for the future if the extraneous

aspects of athletic success could coalesce into the importance of meaningful educational experiences as an end at least equal to the joys of athletic participation.

This analysis demonstrates that the definition of competition and the ability to win cannot be reduced simply to won-lost records and the accumulation of conference and national championships. It is apparent that in certain circumstances individual athletes and athletic teams are essentially competitive and representatively victorious even with modest won-lost laurels. Once all the various factors in the issue are recognized and evaluated, the concept of competition and the ability to win reduces rather simply to a single common denominator: the ability to *compete* or to match individuals and teams against other individuals and teams in a meaningful and reasonably successful manner. As already indicated in numerous ways, this "meaningful and reasonably successful manner" results in degrees of competitiveness ultimately culminating in the accepted standard of success: winning local and national titles and championships. The essential meaning of competition and the ability to win is that individual athletes and athletic teams should never be totally dominated by the league or conference in which they compete. They should not be the proverbial "doormats" and should not be constantly embarrassed by a total inability to *compete* or to play against others in a meaningful and reasonably successful manner. They should realistically expect to win more or less consistently over some individuals and some teams, and they should realistically expect to lose more or less consistently to some more advantaged individuals and teams. This can be related also to the concept of *viability* understood as the general health and well-being of sports programs despite their won-lost records and conference championships. Viability in sports programs is reflected in the attraction such programs consistently have for top-quality athletes who want to be associated with the programs, and in the respect of rival coaches and players and the support of feeder-coaches where this applies. Viability is reflected also in popular acceptance by the local public including student bodies, and perhaps most significantly in the positive feeling of progress and enjoyment on the part of athletes involved in such programs.

COACHING ADEQUACY

The issue of competition and the ability to win can be discussed somewhat more specifically from the perspective of *coaching adequacy*. Probably too little has been said in all of this about the critically important role of coaching and coaches at every level of the sporting enterprise. So much of the dedicated effort and eventual success of individual athletes and sports teams derive from the technical and spiritual contributions of competent and committed coaches, and so much of the heartbreak and frustration of athletic failures so often relates to instances of coaching inadequacy. There are three basic logistical components in every sound and successful sports and athletic program: 1) sufficient and properly utilized financial support in every area of the program; 2) sound and efficient and imaginative administration and direction of the program; and 3) competent and dedicated coaches with technical knowledge of the game and a strong appreciation of the spiritual and humanistic values of sports and athletics. The fourth important factor is talented playing personnel both in quantity and diversity of ability, and such personnel are usually guaranteed through the first three factors reflected in intelligent management planning. These ingredients in themselves and in combination normally result in maximum competitive ability and a winning program, and probably the most critical link in the functional operation of the chain is superior coaching and coaches.

Coaching adequacy can be perceived and measured over a period of time in the context of games and matches that *should be won* by individual athletes and teams in given sports, and games and matches that *could be won or lost* by individual athletes and teams in given sports. The third category involves games and matches against historically and obviously superior opponents whenever this occurs, and these are games and matches which in theory *should be lost*. The empirical factors which combine to determine these winning-losing game categories include: 1) relatively equal financial support for individual athletes and teams in rival sports programs; 2) relatively equal special inducements for the acquisition and retention of playing personnel in rival programs; 3) relatively equal standards and criteria for coaching personnel in rival programs; and 4) relatively equal types and sizes of organization and administration in rival programs. Some aspects of these empirical factors may be relatively difficult to measure (especially the details of financial support including professional salaries and numbers and types of intercollegiate athletic grants-in-aid), but much of this is visible to the naked eye for practiced observers with some statistical ability and resources.

The principle is that coaching is adequate when individual athletes and teams win the games and matches that *should be won*, and win their fair share (at least 50 percent over a period of time) of games and matches that *could be won or lost*. A historical pattern of "upsets" over theoretically stronger opponents and teams naturally is a positive factor and greatly enhances the image of coaching adequacy. Another type of commentary on the measurement of coaching adequacy involves the concept of being "out-coached" by rival coaches when organizational structures and playing personnel and game conditions are relatively equal. This concept relates to such items as: 1) the coach's ability to motivate players generally and for particular games and matches; 2) the coach's ability to have an apparently good game plan and the ability to react to expected and unexpected game developments and personnel changes; and 3) the coach's ability to control the strategic tenor of the game or match to temporary and long-range advantage. The presence and the manifestation of these abilities over a period of time usually constitutes coaching adequacy, and minimizes or eliminates the possibilities and instances of unnecessary defeats. Sound and successful sports and athletic programs are essentially *winning* programs, but theories of competition and the ability to win are complex and must be carefully interpreted to preserve the best interests of participants and the integrity of the sporting enterprise.

CHAPTER EIGHT

The Joy
and the
Triumph

The serious ones say that sports are an escape. It seems far more true to the eye, the ear, the heart, and the mind that history is an escape. Work is an escape. Causes are an escape. Historical movements are an escape. All these escapes must be attempted. . .but the heart of human reality is courage, honesty, freedom, community, excellence: the heart is sports.[1]

M uch has been said in the preceding pages about the values and contributions of sports and athletics in the philosophical and humanistic orientation of human existence. One of the most eloquent and heartfelt commentaries on the subject is Michael Novak's *The Joy of Sports*, a book written with the erudition of an accomplished scholar and the intense enthusiasm of a participant and active spectator. This chapter attempts to capture and convey the spirit and the message of this ebullient hymn of praise to"End Zones, Bases, Baskets, Balls, and the Consecration of the American Spirit." In this addition to his expanding philosophy and theology of culture, Novak contends that sports and athletics constitute the heart of human reality and stand at least equally important in human life along with politics and industry and the arts. He portrays sports and athletics as the "chief civilizing agency in our society and culture," and adds that they comprise the classic form or expression of natural religion. The cogency of his arguments is matched by the poetic brilliance of his expression, and the book is a testament to the honest zeal of an articulate prophet.

Philosophy as a discipline is essentially an attempt to explain or at least to describe the nature of reality in itself and in its various manifestations including *human reality*. Novak's discussion of the "metaphysics of sports" contends that sports and athletics constitute the heart of human reality and all else is diversion and derivation. Contrary to the legacy of the Puritan ethic, play and not work is the essence of our existence—primarily because play ennobles our freedom and produces our values.

> Play, not work, is the end of life. To participate in the rites of play is to dwell in the Kingdom of Ends. To participate in work, career, and the making of history is to labor in the Kingdom of Means. The modern age, the age of history, nourishes illusions. In a Protestent culture, as in Marxist cultures, work is serious, important, adult. Its essential insignificance is overlooked. Work, of course, must be done. But we should be wise enough to distinguish necessity from reality. Play is reality. Work is diversion and escape.
>
> Work is justified by myth: that the essential human task is to improve the world. The vision of history this ideology drums into us, with accompanying trumpet flourish, is the 'march of time.' *Progress*. Our ancestors were inferior to ourselves in knowledge, virtue and civilization. Our present task is to advance the human condition beyond the state in which we find it. That the reality of human life contradicts this myth does not usually disabuse us of it, at least in our conscious minds. What we call progress should, perhaps, be interpreted in exactly the reverse way: *Decline*.[2]

The sense of this is that the vaunted vehicles of progress and civilization, the ostensibly real and serious human pursuits of politics and education and religion, have not really improved the world over the centuries but have simply changed some of our views and perspectives. We may not have forgotten the sins of our fathers, but we are nevertheless condemned to repeat them in new and novel ways. There is no less corruption in politics and government today than in centuries past; our industrialized society provides materialistic benefits undreamed of in earlier times, but the cost is the loss of significant human values and essential dimensions in human existence: "concentration of energy, simplicity and inner definition." Modern science has enhanced the quality of life in many ways, but has also provided bigger and better ways of destroying ourselves in the short-range and long-range scheme of things. "I would not want to stand before God and claim to be better than my ancestors."

Sports and Athletics as the Fundamental Reality

Sports and athletics constitute the fundamental reality because they are the source and the bastion of the most important human values of "courage and honesty and freedom and community and excellence." These are what we strive to inculcate in every facet of our lives including the work-world, and their clearest and most consistent expression is the world of sports and athletics. This is the sense in which sports and athletics constitute "the chief civilizing agency in our society and culture." More people in our society learn the values of civilization from sports and athletics than from any other single source of cultural formation. As indicated earlier, our society and culture reflect and are based on meritorious *agon* or worthy struggle and competition directed to the achievement of human excellence in every sphere. In the context of Novak's analysis, the achievement of human excellence is the recognition and practice of the fundamental human values of courage, honesty, freedom, community, and excellence; and these are portrayed more publicly and more consistently in sports and athletics than in any other facet of our social structure. These fundamental values exist of course in other areas including politics, education, and religion, but the point is that more people come to perceive and appreciate these values through sports and athletics than any other cultural medium. In our society and culture, sports and athletics are much more visible to more people and have a far greater impact than more traditional incubators of human values including the arts and BBC television, and this for the simple reason that many more millions of people in our society and culture enshrine Super Bowls and World Series and Stanley Cups rather than Nobel prizes and symphonies and works of art.[3]

> Sports are at the heart of the matter. Sports are the high point of civilization—along with the arts, but more powerfully than the arts, which are special in taste and execution and appeal. . . .
>
> Sports are not, of course, all of life. What good are courage, honesty, freedom, community, and excellence if they do not inform one's family life, civic life, political life, work life? Sports do not celebrate such qualities in order to contain them, but in order to hold them clearly before the aspiring heart. . . .What the person of wisdom needs to derive from every sphere of life is its inherent beauty, attraction, power, force. . . .
>
> Sports are as old as the human race. Sports are the highest products of civilization and the most accessible, lived and experiential sources of the civilizing spirit. In sports, law was born and also liberty, and the nexus of their interrelation. In sports, honesty and excellence are caught, captured, nourished, held in trust for generations. . . .The mind at play, the body at play—these furnish our imaginations with the highest achievements of beauty the human race attains. Symphonies, statues, novels, poems, dances, essays, philosophical treatises—these are transpositions of the world of sports into the exercises of human civilization. Sports are their fundament, their never-failing life source. Cease play, cease civilization. Work is the diversion necessary for play to survive.[4]

Sports and athletics are not the only important concerns in human life, but they are *equally* important and perhaps more fundamental compared to commonly accepted and culturally approved media for displaying and enacting the essence of humanity. As indicated earlier, commentators on the human scene have long extolled the scholar and the intellectual for their contributions to the progress and well-being of mankind, but the humanizing and civilizing capacity and role of sports and athletics has generally been mistakenly ignored and unfairly minimized. "It is fashionable to put down 'jocks.'

Others, of course, put down businessmen, or do-gooders, or beatniks, or artists, or theologians, or secularists, or saints. It is part of the human comedy for everyone to put down someone." In a strong and pointed commentary "which my editors and even my wife urged me to modify or eliminate," Novak describes one of his own "biases" about the importance of sports and athletics in the fabric of humanity.

> Those who have contempt for sports, our serious citizens, are a danger to the human race, ants among men, drones in the honeycomb. . . .
>
> I have never met a person who disliked sports, or who absented himself or herself entirely from them, who did not at the same time seem to me deficient in humanity. . . .I mean that a quality of sensitivity, an organ of perception, an access to certain significant truths appear to be missing. Such persons seem to me a danger to civilization. I do not, on the whole, like to work with them. In their presence I find myself on guard, often unconsciously. I expect from them a certain softness of mind, from their not having known a sufficient number of defeats. Unless they have compensated for it elsewhere, I anticipate that they will underestimate the practice and discipline required for execution, or the role of chance and Fate in human outcomes. I expect them to have a view of the world far too rational and mechanical.[5]

In the interests of balance and the true picture, it must be emphasized that personal deficiencies relating to the proper appreciation of sports and athletics constitute just one of numerous and diverse possiblities for deficiencies in the human spirit. People who dislike or have no regard or intelligent interest in the arts and politics and religion are also seriously lacking in the components of humanity. The problem is that these aesthetic and intellectual deficiencies are quickly recognized and constantly deplored, while the equally significant sins of omission relating to an appreciation of sports and athletics are largely unrecognized and often misinterpreted. This is due primarily to the kind of widespread misunderstanding of the philosophical and humanistic values and contributions of sports and athletics that books such as this are intended to correct. Perhaps it is due most specifically to the common failure to recognize in a responsible way the importance and the dignity of physical excellence along with spiritual perfection in human existence. The world of sports and athletics is a valid and legitimate sphere of human activity (not just "animal occupation"), and historically and naturally constitutes an acceptable place to live and move and have our being.

Sports and athletics are more than the pastimes of childhood and adolescence—they are serious human pursuits at any age whose depth, intensity, and capacity for humanistic growth simply increase in the maturity of adulthood. The values of sports and athletics are the values of life and a lifetime, and befit and enhance the sagacity of age even more than they provide for the joys of youth. Nor is it valid to say with simplistic critics and detractors that "it's only a game and don't take it so seriously." It is always more than a game—except in the sense that life itself is a game and a serious game with the highest risks and the greatest prize. In what is probably the most fundamental context available to mind and pen, Novak suggests that the metaphysical reality of sports and athletics is the metaphysical reality of life and death.

> For the underlying metaphysics of sports entails overcoming the fear of death. In every contest, one side is defeated. Defeat hurts. No use saying 'it's only a game.' It doesn't feel like a game. The anguish and depression that seize one's psyche in defeat are far deeper than a mere comparative failure—deeper than recognition of the opponent's superiority. . .A game tests considerably more than talent. A game tests, somehow, one's entire life. It tests one's standing with fortune and the gods. Defeat is too like death. Defeat hurts like death. . . .
>
> How can that be? How can a mere game be a combat with death? But it is. One knows it. One's body knows it. One's

psyche knows it. . .Sports are not diversion. Entertainment diverts. A contest rivets the energies of life on a struggle for survival. . .To win an athletic contest is to feel as though the gods are on one's side, as though one is Fate's darling, as if the powers of being course through one's veins and radiate from one's actions—powers stronger than non-being, powers over ill fortune, powers over death. Victory is abundant life, vivacity, bubbling over. Defeat is silence, withdrawal, passivity, glumness.

Each time one enters a contest, one's unseen antagonist is death. Not one's visible opponent, who is only the occasion for the struggle. But the Negative Spirit, the Denier. That is why the image of the aging athlete is so poignant: it begins to mix the ritual contest with the actual contest, ritual death with the coming of real death. In the aging athlete, the ultimate reality of sports breaks through the symbol, becomes explicit. . .Human life is essentially a defeat; we die. The victories of sport are ritual triumphs of grace, agility, perfection, beauty over death.[6]

Sports and Athletics as Natural Religion

This comprehensive recognition of the philosophical and humanistic dimensions of sports and athletics extends into the equally significant theological and religious areas of human experience. Properly evaluated and interpreted, the world of sports and athletics has a remarkably evident religious character comparable in scope and detail to traditional religious concepts and practices. In his chapter on sports and athletics as "The Natural Religion," Novak describes and explains the omnipresent and yet largely unappreciated religious quality of sports and athletics. One of his analogies is the notion of a spaceship from an alien planet hovering over our earth on fall weekends, observing the curious spectacle of hundreds of thousands of people gathered in vast oval "temples of female goddesses" intently participating in some form of ritual or ceremony performed on large green altars. On closer inspection, the interplanetary visitors peer into individual dwellings and see clusters of other worshippers huddled around smaller altars, reverently and silently absorbed in versions of the ritual or ceremony. The visitors would most probably conclude that they had discovered a particularly religious civilization in which much of the population regularly pays homage to immensely respected religious deities.

The premise in arguing that sports and athletics comprise a form of natural religion is that religious fervor and religious belief occur in a variety of forums beyond the traditional or biblical denominations. There are secular and civil expressions of faith and belief and sacred trust which include all the substance and pageantry of traditional religions. An event of recent memory in American society is the political conventions in the summer of 1980, and these provide a ready and classic example of civil religiosity full of pomp and ceremony and dedicated commitment to the chosen Saviours of our way of life, to the modern prophets who alone can bring down the tablets from the mountaintop to guide us in the preservation of morality and decency and show us the promise of the future. Human spirituality and our quest for godliness and holiness are expressed in many aspects of human experience beyond the walls of our churches and synagogues. Man by nature is a lover and a believer in mystical perfections perceived and pursued through prescribed rituals with intense faith and hope in the triumph of the good.[7]

It is in this sense that sports and athletics express the classic natural religion of the past and present, with all the design and purpose and special accoutrements of traditional religions. Traditional religions are lived and expressed in rituals and symbolism, and the world of sports and athletics is intensely ritualistic and symbolic. The sports ceremony is dramatically staged in *sacred space* (athletic cathedrals) and *sacred time* (the time of the heroes), and begins with the mandatory opening hymn and carefully orchestrated entrance parades by the participants. Definite and recognizable roles are assigned and carried out by the hierarchy of participants and the spectator-worshippers, and the event is played out with reverent emotion typical of religious spectacles. The fundamental symbolism of sports and athletics has already been established: it is the symbolism of life and death through winning and losing. Losing is like death but winning is life itself, and to win is to be reborn with all the significance of baptisms and bar mitzvahs and other rites of passage exalted in traditional religious dogma and practice.

Traditional religions obviously require faith and belief in the activity itself and in the God or gods who define the religious experience. Sports and athletics also require faith and belief in the possibility of personal salvation through the achievement of human excellence. One of the operative distinctions in Novak's analysis hinges on the concept of *belief* applied in an essentially religious context. He contends that advocates of sports and athletics are *believers*, and people who reject sports and athletics are nonbelievers. As in disputes over the validity and acceptability of traditional religious belief, the gulf between the two camps is significant and attempts at dialogue are often futile and frustrating. The experience of belief in general is sometimes difficult to articulate in universally meaningful terms, and believers and nonbelievers are left largely to their own convictions with little room for common ground. As with Catholics and Protestants who cannot understand why non-Catholics and non-Protestants willingly turn away from truth and salvation, so believers in sports and athletics do not understand how detractors and disparagers can fail to appreciate the values and ideals of the well-played game. In traditional religion and also in sports and athletics, believers do not really *blame* nonbelievers and frequently exert time and energy in evangelizing and proselytizing to help nonbelievers perceive the true and the good.

Traditional religion is naturally value-oriented and catechistically concerned with ethics and morality, and sports and athletics are equally value-oriented and are routinely measured by their adherence to ethical and moral principles and purposes. It has already been established that sports and athletics comprise the most fertile source of human values such as courage, honesty, freedom, community, and excellence. This axiological aspect provokes justifiable concern about integrity and a sense of probity in sports and athletics, and this explains the profound disillusionment and public indignation that follow revelations of cheating and dishonesty in the sporting enterprise. Somehow it should never happen here—in politics or in business perhaps, or wherever, but never in the sacred halls of athletic competition where only skill and will and Fate prevail. It should never happen in this unique area of human activity that is the origin and the model of our concepts of *fairness* and *unfairness*, of playing by the rules of life and the rules of the game, of doing what is right and avoiding what is wrong.

Traditional religions have their hierarchies of deities and sacred personnel, beginning with concepts of God and including saints or persons of consecrated memory, and also functioning dignitaries such as priests, ministers, and rabbis. Sports and athletics have similar hierarchies beginning with the unnamed but commonly accepted divinities of the game, the gods and goddesses of fortune and fate who turn the mystical wheels of victory and defeat and shine their light on the good performances and the good seasons. The saints of sports and athletics are the sports figures of heroic proportion and hallowed memory—the Knute Rocknes, the Red Granges, the Babe Ruths, the Walter Hagens, the chosen few who are legends in their own time and forevermore. The functioning dignitaries are the players and managers and coaches who conduct the sporting rituals, and minister in their own way to the clamoring needs of the faithful in the stands. Even here sports and athletics parallel religious festivals: religious dignitaries wear priestly vestments befitting their office and setting them apart from the congregation, and so too the dignitaries of sports and athletics wear colorful uniforms to mark their priestly stature. And a final comparison is that both religion and sports and athletics emphasize self-denial and bodily sacrifice in the name of spiritual achievement and human excellence. Most of us shy away from voluntary ordeal and pain and suffering, but athletes (and saints) are unique in seeking out such experiences and deliberately "making it hurt" for the sake of transcendent values and goals.

Sports and athletics reflect the matter and form of religious organization and religious devotion. In his testament to the religiosity of sports and athletics, Novak lists the spiritual essentials common to both areas:

> . . .Sports flow outward into action from a deep natural impulse that is radically religious: an impulse of freedom, respect for ritual limits, a zest for symbolic meaning, and a longing for perfection. The athlete may of course be pagan, but sports are. . .natural religions. There are many ways to express this radical impulse: by the aesthetics and dedication of preparation; by a sense of respect for the mysteries of one's own body and soul, and for powers not in one's own control; by a sense of awe for the place and time of competition; by a sense of fate; by a felt sense of comradeship and destiny; by a sense of participation in the rhythms and tides of nature itself.[8]

All this bespeaks the spiritual richness of serious athletic participation. Nor is it viable to contend that sports and athletics cannot be religious because of the cynicism and skepticism of internal and external critics: this too is an intrinsic mark of organized religion through the ages. Cynicism, skepticism, and irreverence are the other side of the religious coin, and such attitudes meld into the religious experience for the individual and for the institution. It can be maintained that constructive criticism is the life-blood of emerging and established human (and divine) institutions.

> A religion without skeptics is like a bosom never noticed. . . . When Catholicism goes sour, as periodically down the centuries it does, almost always the reason is a dearth of critics, or worse, the death of heretics. A nonprophet church decays. When things go well, it is because critics condemn what is going on. A decent religion needs irreverence as meat needs salt.[9]

The depth and credence of institutions in society are directly proportionate to the depth and credence of the values and commitments they generate, and this is the common measure of sports and athletics and the religious experience.

Breaking the Seals: The Bond of Brothers

Novak contends that ". . . Seven seals lock the inner life of sports. They may be broken, one by one."[10] These seven seals are *sacred space* and *sacred time*; *the bond of brothers*; *rooting and agon*; and *competing and self-discovery*. (Sacred space, sacred time, and rooting were discussed earlier in other contexts—see chapters II and III.) The *bond of brothers* is one of the truly beautiful aspects of sports and athletics, with implications and consequences for one of mankind's most elusive quests: the search for androgyny. It is curiously true that the often violent world of sports and athletics is a place also of compassion and altruism and a kind of love rarely seen in the rest of society. Emotional displays between males especially and even females are usually discouraged and misunderstood in our social and cultural contexts, where roles and models for the sexes are firmly fixed and deviation brings suspicion. Sports and athletics break the mold and bare natural emotions and generate the mutual love and respect known only to comrades in heroic struggle. Males and females cry openly in the euphoria of victory and the sorrow of defeat. Athletes embrace in the inexpressible joy of noble ideals achieved, and in the silent compassion of sacrifices wasted, dreams destroyed, and the emptiness of loss. It is interesting that similar demonstrations outside sports and athletics typically involve life and death in reality and in symbol: births, funerals, happy reunions, and sad farewells. In the world of sports and athletics, they are equally intense and much more frequent and often displayed for generations to appreciate.

> . . . Millions of men look back nostalgically on their days in active athletics precisely because they experienced there, as at few other points in their lives, a quality of tenderness, a stream of

caring and concern from and toward others, such as would make the most ardent imaginers of the androgynous ideal envious. Male bonding is one of the most paradoxical forms of human tenderness: harsh, sweet, gentle, abrupt, soft . . . Among men, sports help to form a brotherhood for which, alas, sisterhood has no similar equivalent, and which it is a high human imperative to invent.

Androgynous? Why do critics so often leer that 'jocks' are secret homosexuals, patting one another's buttocks, showing off their well-angled forearms and thighs, affectionately joshing one another in the showers. Sports bring out in every ideal team a form of gentleness and tenderness so intense that it is no misnomer to call it love; and coaches commonly speak to their supposed macho males like golden-tongued preachers of love, brotherhood, comradeship. Tears, burning throats, and raw love of male for male are not unknown among athletes in the daily heat of preparation . . . and in the solemn battle. In the working world, such tears must normally await the testimonial dinner upon retirement. They are wrong who think the 'brains' are androgynous and the jocks afflicted with machismo. For gentleness of demeanor, I will take the athlete eight times out of ten. For hardness of heart, I have learned to fear the man who has always hated sports.[11]

The history and the world of sports and athletics are rich with examples. Who can fail to be moved by the love and brotherhood in legendary Notre Dame football star George Gipp's death-bed request to Knute Rockne (even if dramatically embellished over the years): "Someday when the going is rough, tell them to win one for the Gipper, and wherever I am I'll know it and be happy." How many millions cried along with Lou Gehrig and Babe Ruth in their poignant farewells to baseball and to life. Who could fail to appreciate the special feeling and mutual caring and manly love in the violent world of Vince Lombardi's Green Bay Packer football dynasty. What story of true compassion and tenderness can compare with the relationship of professional football players Gale Sayers and Brian Piccolo prior to the tragic finale depicted in *Brian's Song*. How many opinions were changed when tough and blasé Al McGuire wept openly after his Marquette University basketball team won the NCAA national championship in his last year of coaching. How many hearts responded to Nadia Comaneci's innocent joy and radiant happiness after her first Olympic triumphs. What vignette can match the misty-eyed embrace of seasoned professionals Paul Owens and Dallas Green after their long-thwarted Philadelphia Phillies won the 1980 World Series. And who can forget or fail to thrill to the inspiring display of love and shared fulfillment by the 1980 U.S. Olympic hockey team after their classic victories in Lake Placid.

AGON AND COMPETITION

Agon and *competition* are the essence of sports and athletics and the essence of human existence and experience. The philosophy of sports and athletics is the philosophy of life itself: life since the biblical fall is a test and a trial and the constant confrontation of challenging alternatives. *Agon* characterizes our hopes and enlivens our dreams, and defines the human spirit in the quest for satisfaction and the achievement of excellence.

> Sports are creations of the human spirit, arenas of the human spirit, instructors of the human spirit, arts of the human spirit. Spirit is not always visible in sports; is not always actualized; is often dormant. But at any moment it may flash through. . .In any one game, a man cannot count on being given opportunities for greatness; over a season, or over a lifetime, the opportunities are finite, can be numbered, come at their own pace. Thus one must be ever alert to grab greatness as it passes by—to seize every risk, accept every dare. The great ones attempt what the good ones let go by. This, too, is a window to the spirit.
>
> If I had to give one single reason for my love of sports it would be this: I love the tests of the human spirit. . . .[12]

Competition is the expression of *agon* in sports and athletics and in life itself. It was contended earlier that ours is a society of intense competition where winning is important (sometimes too important), and where we constantly measure supremacy in various ways. We all want to be number one.

> Political leaders, foundation executives, and professors—by no means all such, but of a certain disposition—hate to lose. Not only because defeat is death, but also because being number two does not suit them. Upwardly mobile America is fiercely competitive, in an abstract way: what matters is not substance but competitive position. . . .[13]

There are many reasons why we want to win, and various views of what victory means. Some see winning in financial terms: a higher salary now and a higher base for the rest of one's life. Some revel in being the best—in living on top of the mountain and looking down at the rest. Some relate winning as the blessing of Fate and the natural reward for destiny's darlings. Some see winning as the ultimate expression of personal achievement and the mastery of others in the mastery of oneself.[14] Everyone's shining hour is to combine all these with balance and integrity in the final triumph of the human spirit.

Sports and athletics and life itself have similar aims, purposes, and goals. To play and to live as flawlessly as possible and to give the ultimate performance draws us to competitive struggles and the chance to win.

> Those who deplore (and secretly dread) the intense competitiveness of American life might observe: 1) that during a lifetime, as during a career, one must expect to lose often; to die many times with grace is excellent preparation for reality; 2) that there is a difference in desiring harmony between one's best performance and the laurels of Good Fortune and desiring to vanquish an opponent; and 3) that every once in a while, the humiliation of an arrogant opponent is an immensely satisfying and highly democratic pleasure, not to be ascetically declined. . . .[15]

SELF-DISCOVERY AND SELF-REVELATION

Self-discovery is one of the subtle mysteries and most valuable rewards of sports and athletics. Few other areas of human activity provide the means and the opportunity for such immediate and measureable self-revelation and self-knowledge at the physical and emotional and intellectual levels. And in few other areas is the information to oneself and to others so quickly perceived and so publicly judged. The concept of *unalienated action* was used in an earlier context and applies here as well: there is a clarity and openness in sports and athletics rarely seen in other forms of human activity. Sports and athletics involve a kind of activity best described as unambiguous and unequivocal, in which meanings and purposes are evident and the instruments of achievement are known to one and all. More than most other practitioners of human arts, athletes are vulnerable to the nakedness of the spirit individually and collectively.

One of the values of self-discovery through sports and athletics is its truly inner-directed character consistent with the most profound religious experiences. In the same way as the philosopher Martin Heidegger says that we discover "Being in the emptiness of Nothingness," we discover ourselves in discovering our inner limits: in discovering what we are not and perhaps can never be.[16] Competition is the key to this kind of self-discovery: in the purity of serious competition, we push ourselves to our limits and come to know ourselves in the context of what we can do.

> In will and intention, each athlete knows perfection. The vast majority cannot come close to attaining it. Every athlete in every sport discovers very early that others, in this way or that, are his superior . . . Each must, sooner or later, cease pretending to be what he is not, cannot be, and rejoice in playing up to the limit given him. Life is not equal. God is no egalitarian. . .
>
> A great rival is a great gift. How can one extend oneself into fresh heights if there is no one to force one higher? An artist of any sort who has no peers suffers from the lack. Great peers

make one greater than one could become in solitude. When I have tried and tried, again and again, and still cannot keep abreast of my rival, there comes, perhaps, disappointment, even grief, but finally reconciliation. My limits have been extended to the breaking point. I can go no further. Thanks, friend; otherwise, how would I know?

Yet the recognition of limits is not the only form of maturation taught by sports. There comes also, at least to some, a sense of their own bodies and attitudes, a sense as it were *from the inside out*, quiet, subtle, full of luminosity and peacefulness, beaming from deep within until its rays at last reach consciousness: a sense of inner unity. *Distinguer pour unir*. . . In certain combinations, one's body and heart and soul seem to move as one, and one's performances improve. Learning how to listen for the fertile self, the united self, is as important for the athlete as for the writer.[17]

This is the power, the glory, and the mystique of sports and athletics. This is the spiritual joy and the spiritual fulfillment of thought and action uniquely united in the sporting experience as the ultimate paradigm of life itself.

Trying to capture the spirit and the message of *The Joy of Sports* is like trying to capture the wind, and the reason is simple enough: there is a *world* at issue here, a fine and noble world of fire and ice and truth and meaning. The world of sports and athletics is the human and humanizing world— the realm of courage, honesty, freedom, community, and excellence, rich and deep in lasting significance and possibilities for self-realization and caring, and superbly stable and enduring.

The older one gets, the more the Serious Issues seem to be the highest comedy of all. And the more basic and fundamental seem to be the realities of sport: community, courage, harmony of mind and body, beauty, and excellence. Let New Moralities come, and Old Moralities be despised; still, three strikes and you're out, and a base hit when your buddies need it is a deed of beauty.[18]

CHAPTER NINE

The Future
of
Sports and
Athletics

Along with prostitution and espionage (and generally less rewarding than either of these), the third oldest human profession is prognosticating the future in human affairs. Attempts to transcend the space-time limitations of human intelligence and imagination abound in the efforts of groups and individuals throughout history to our own times, and constantly deploy the powers of creative speculation against the edges of accuracy. Projecting the future of sports and athletics is fraught with the same difficulties inherent in forecasting the future in other areas of human activity. In the context of this book's contention that sports and athletics are essential and definitive in human existence and experience, it is intriguing that a contemporary dramatic prediction for the demise of our world involves a futuristic form of sports and athletics. The film *Rollerball* depicts the usurpation of sports and athletics by the "ultimate corporate conglomerates," and the systematic utilization of athletic teams to wage the final brutal battles to destroy civilization. The prospect is foreboding for many reasons—not the least of them the possibility that sports and athletics would be subordinated to such pernicious socioeconomic designs.[1]

In search of a base for projections about the future of sports and athletics, the following principles are inherent in the broad prologue to what will be: 1) sports and athletics constitute a microcosm of society and will continue to reflect social and cultural attitudes and developments; 2) the spirit of *agon-alea* (competition and chance) is intrinsic in human experience and will prevail unless totally destroyed by life-altering innovations in the name of sociopolitical control (George Orwell's *1984* carried to the highest power); and 3) in the apocolyptic event of the destruction of civilization as we know it, the signs of its renaissance will be renewed forms of friendly competition among people and nations.[2]

Projections or speculations about the future of sports and athletics emerge from at least three basic areas or categories relating to the sporting enterprise in the context of sociocultural developments. The first area is the *functional* or *structural* area comprising physical and pragmatic innovations in the nature and organization of sports and athletics. The second area is the "great reformation" area designed to eliminate or at least minimize current abuses and corruptions in sports and athletics at every level. The third area is the *cosmic* or *futuristic* area comprising scientific and technological innovations with far-reaching consequences for civilization and its components including sports and athletics.

Functional and Structural Innovations

The *functional* or *structural* area relates to projections about physical conditions and organizational structures in the future of sports and athletics. The first probability here is that weather and the seasonal character of sports and athletics will become things of the past. The portent is the current existence and popularity of domed and semi-domed stadiums for traditional outdoor sports: baseball, football, soccer, and track and field. There are several such facilities already in use (the best-known are the Astrodome in Houston and the Superdome in New Orleans), and this is the trend of the future. The result will be a national and perhaps even international network of all-weather facilities eliminating cold, heat, wind, and rain as factors in the sporting experience. All this will come at the price of some nostalgia, since it will mean the end of traditional wintry and windy conditions for football and soccer and the grand American tradition of baseball in the summer sun. Some sports will forever be pursued under the supernal dome of nature: golf, surfing, mountain-climbing, and others where the sky is literally the limit.

With the elimination of the weather factor for many sports, the hallowed seasonal character of sports and athletics will also pass into history. Given the interest of participants and spectators (and this could constitute a critical given), many popular sports could be played at any time of the calendar year—or all through the calendar year. The seasonal character of traditional sports has already been stretched beyond original time frames: professional basketball extends from September to June; professional baseball begins in effect in March and ends in October; professional football stretches from August to January; ice hockey is played from October to May; and many intercollegiate sports are virtually year-round enterprises. The availability of scientifically perfected weather-proofed stadiums will add to this trend, and traditional seasons for many sports will become memories along with stadium coats and bleacher tans.

Another aspect of this functional area or category concerns the future organizational structure of sports and athletics with respect to geographical expansion. The geographical expansion of professional sports franchises in leagues and conferences is one of the most evident and sometimes most troublesome aspects of sports history over the past two or three decades. Leagues and conferences in professional baseball, football, basketball, and hockey have expanded beyond expectations in recent years, vastly increasing the number of teams and participants and pools of spectators in this country and in other countries. This expansion is likely to continue and intensify, and will lead to a larger (forty teams in some leagues) and more decentralized sports structure. This development probably will run the risk of over-saturation in various areas, and will have to be handled intelligently to avoid self-destruction. Depending to some extent on the realization of more numerous indoor facilities described earlier, expansion in sports and athletics is likely to reflect our national population shifts to "follow the sun" and move from northern and eastern cities into the south and west. Sports franchises and programs will follow suit, and future sports strongholds might well shift from the traditional Bostons and New Yorks and Chicagos to the Miamis and Tempes and El Pasos.

Future expansion in sports and athletics is also likely to extend beyond our national borders into other countries depending on the nature and popularity of various sports, and we could well see the formation of global conferences and leagues in selected sports. Soccer has long prided iteself on its international character, and this is perhaps the one popular sport in which the United States is inferior in status and player development compared to other countries. Professional ice hockey has always reflected worldwide interest, and baseball could easily move into such historically receptive countries as Japan, Mexico, and South and Central America. Many European countries and the Soviet Union have indicated considerable interest in basketball and have already established a network of semiprofessional teams in Italy, Germany, Spain, and the Netherlands, stocked to some extent by American college players. American intercollegiate teams in football, basketball, and baseball have played exhibition games in foreign countries with increasing frequency. Professional and amateur golf and tennis for decades have staged international events including some of the most prestigious championships in the sporting world, and horse-racing historically and traditionally has been the sport of kings in every land. Renewed interest in the international aspects of Olympic competition and world-wide recognition of the importance of the Games will serve as another stimulus in the global expansion of sports and athletics.

"Great Reformations" in Sports and Athletics

The "great reformation" area or category of predictions and speculations about sports and athletics is the most pressing in the context of contemporary concern about the viable future of the sporting enterprise. Much has been said in this study about potential and real abuses and corruptions in intercollegiate and professional sports and athletics, and the need for constructive reform is pressing and obvious. In both the intercollegiate and professional areas, abuses and corruptions (and therefore reforms) are related to the economic implications and consequences of the "win at all costs" syndrome. This makes predictions and plans for reform multifaceted and complicated, and eventually dependent on socioeconomic attitudes beyond the immediate context of the sports world. As indicated in earlier discussions of this phenomenon, sports and athletics tend to repeat the ills of a secular and mercenary society dedicated to winning at all costs. A sociocultural spiritual renewal resulting in more aesthetic values and goals would change the situation, but this is probably more of an ideal than a practical reality.

Unfortunately for society and for sports and athletics, a more immediate reaction to the rampant professionalism in sports and athletics is something mentioned earlier in another context (in chapter I): public indignation and condemnation culminating eventually in government intervention and control. Such public disillusionment would compromise the intrinsic values and virtues of sports and athletics, and would (at least temporarily) blunt the potential for good in authentically oriented sporting experiences. The spectre of governmental control is particularly distasteful since it militates against the essence of sports and athletics as the supremely free expression of the human spirit. Any kind of legislative control is futile and self-defeating in the truly definitive areas of human existence and experience: in morality and the need for moral choice; in aesthetic preference and personal allegiances; in the nature and manifestation of religious belief; in the perception of happiness and how to achieve it; and in the freedom to play as the ultimate prerogative of mankind expressing humanity. All this is so tellingly evident in totalitarian countries where freedom is suppressed and violated, and perhaps most evident in the government *business* of sports and athletics in such countries. Sports and athletics exist in such regimes, but they are corrupted into the world of work and seriousness and the struggle for international political supremacy. Let the time never come when American sports and athletics are so perverted as to become an extension of political regimentation rather than the inalienable right of free citizens.

Since sports and athletics reflect trends and themes in our socioeconomic structure, the sporting enterprise will follow economic indicators and situations wherever these lead for society in general. Our current inflationary spiral is represented in sports and athletics in excessive professional salaries and intercollegiate financial investments, and future variations or deviations (including economic catastrophes) will be copied in the sporting enterprise. Hopefully our economy will stabilize in a realistic balance of expenses and incomes, and thereby avoid the economic disasters of inflation run wild and/or another Great Depression with all the dire consequences for every social segment including sports and athletics.[3] It is significant that sports and athletics show a stubborn history through serious economic trials: in the depths of the Great Depression the sports stadiums were filled and Babe Ruth's $80,000 salary in a time of economic destitution for many was accepted as a part of life and a part of the game. The lure of the sporting spirit prevails in the best of times and the worst of times.

While much of the preceding analysis relates primarily to professional sports and athletics, the intercollegiate scene also reflects our socioeconomic attitudes in the context of constructive reforms. The most destructive aspect of contemporary sports and athletics is the professionalizing of many intercollegiate programs in the name of winning—because "winning is the only thing" and the reason for this is financial prosperity. As suggested earlier, this is particularly disenchanting since it compromises the noble values and goals of the educational process and the hallowed mandate of colleges and universities. In this area especially the most effective reform would be a reorientation or renewed recognition of spiritual and humanistic values and goals in an age of secular diversion, and thankfully the prospects for such reform in this particular area are more realistic and theoretically more attainable (this will be discussed later in this analysis).

Radical Reformations: Student-Athletes as Professionals

A radically different type of reform for intercollegiate sports and athletics has been suggested periodically by a variety of commentators, and this is the contention that major intercollegiate sports programs (especially major football and basketball programs) should be recognized as professional enterprises and developed as such with minimal acknowledgement of the educational character of colleges and universities. One of the more intelligent and detailed plans of this sort is proposed by James Michener in his *Sports in America*. [4] Michener summarizes the rationale for his proposal in the following statement:

> It is quite obvious that intercollegiate football and basketball, as now played, are semi-professional sports in most schools and professional in others. This should be publicly acknowledged; I see nothing to be gained by denying it and much to be lost. My concern is therefore how best to administer a professional entertainment program within the normal guidelines that now operate, and I would wish to hear no complaint that 'Things oughtn't to be this way in a self-respecting institution of higher learning,' because they are that way and our society intends that they remain that way. We are faced with a *fait accompli*, but we can administer it somewhat better than we are now doing. [5]

Michener is quite right in asserting that "things shouldn't be this way but they are because society wants them this way," but the popular notion that sports and athletics are "professional entertainment" is dubious and needs to be properly interpreted. In their essential purposes and intentions and practiced with probity and integrity, sports and athletics are not entertainment—they never have been and they never will be. Entertainment is diversion and escape—entertainment leaves no residue and contributes nothing to the meaning and the structure of the good life. In the contemporary television milieu, entertainment is *Happy Days* and *Hollywood Squares*, and *Dallas* and *General Hospital*. Entertainment is something one experiences and enjoys and walks away from with never a backward glance or a second thought. Entertainment does not contribute to life except for the enjoyment of the moment (which has its own merit—for the moment). As indicated in the previous chapter, sports and athletics are *not* diversion and escape: sports are at the heart of human reality and provide humanity's most definitive expression. The problem is that some administrators of contemporary sports programs have violated the essential purposes and intentions of sports and athletics, and have diverted the entire enterprise into an area for which it was never intended and where it cannot function with holistic efficiency. The pathway to sanity and perspective in sports and athletics is not to change the nature of the sporting enterprise to mere entertainment, but to eliminate the diversionary tendencies which violate its character as a definitive dimension in human existence and human values.

Michener's plan would divide "America's 695 colleges and universities" into four groups with corresponding emphasis on professional sports participation as opposed to academic involvement and achievement.

> Group One would consist of those schools who wished to compete in a super-league, with all its television contracts, bowl games and national publicity. In these schools . . . players would be paid a salary for performing, and I would think they might therefore want to be unionized, as are the members of dance bands which play at college festivals. . . .
>
> Group Two would be comprised of . . . universities that wished to remain in conferences, play major schedules with teams of their own calibre, and distribute scholarships to athletes of promise but not quite skilled enough to be hired by schools in Group One. . . .[6]

Groups Three and Four would consist of schools that wish to provide football (and other sports) as entertainment or recreation, but without athletic scholarships and without large coaching staffs or other athletic expenses. In the area of educational opportunity and academic progress, Michener proposes that the "professional hires" in Group One and the realistic scholarship recipients in Group Two should take "only one academic course during the season when his sport is being emphasized." He contends that "the testimony of former players is overwhelming" that serious intercollegiate sports participation is incompatible with normal five-course study loads, and "a realistic solution would be to limit the professional to one course, which would keep him in touch with the academic community in a way that permitted some success." The corollary is that salaries for the professional hires and athletic scholarships should be extended routinely to five years, with the fifth year reserved for the completion of degree requirements postponed from preceding years. "To use an athlete for four years and then chuck him aside with no degee is contemptible."[7]

In a lighter vein of proposals for recognizing the *status quo* in intercollegiate sports programs, Professor John M. Stevens (California State University at Hayward) "carries fears about abuses in scholastic athletics to their logical (?) conclusion" in his presumably facetious article "How To Train and Educate Professional Football Players" (September 1980).[8] Stevens suggests the enactment of a California-based "Football Reform Act" to fund "four professional training centers (administered) by the Vocational Education Office of the State Superintendent of Public Instruction."

> Each center shall employ no more than 250 trainees each year. The centers will operate a year-round program of vigorous training and competition designed to prepare successful professional football players as quickly and efficiently as possible. Trainees will not enroll in academic degree programs. Their pay will be the same as that of assistant professors at the University of California. . .

> These centers would be best administered by the four major California football powers. Stanford, the University of Southern California, and the Berkeley and Los Angeles branches

of the University of California already have the requisite facilities and coaching staffs. The only necessity would be to separate administration of the new centers from that of the academic programs of the four institutions. Since there has always been *de facto* separation, it should be no problem to make this arrangement legal. . . .[9]

Steven's plan would delay the *education* of professionally trained football players until their retirement from the sport. "The California Commission on Postsecondary Education is authorized to spend $1 million on research and development grants to colleges and universities designing programs for the liberal education of retired football players."

> For too long we have assumed that liberal education is some kind of bad-tasting medicine that students must be forced to swallow in their first two years of college. We have foolishly made it a prerequisite for academic or professional specialization. There is precious little empirical evidence that this order of study makes for better specialists and no evidence at all that it results in a liberally educated class of college graduates.

> By reversing the order and providing specialized training first, with liberal education saved for those who have established their roles in the economic order, we might discover that the study of great books, great ideas, great issues—whatever constitutes liberal education in this generation—would not have to be forced on anyone.[10]

Serious proposals along these lines (such as Michener's and others) are tempting to consider in a pragmatic sense, but they involve a kind of capitulation to the givens that we can ill afford. Our sociocultural structure includes certain givens in terms of which we live and act, and some givens are more fundamental and more acceptable than others. Michener points out that the professionalizing of intercollegiate athletics is a *fait accompli* and society wants things to stay this way. The question of right and wrong still exists: it is one thing to recognize the existence of wrong-doing and error and sin, but quite another thing to condone this (implicitly or explicitly) and attempt to build on the situation in the hopes of improving the human condition. This is reminiscent of an exchange of remarks in a recent government committee hearing on violence in professional ice hockey. A representative of the sport contended that permitting fist-fights between players is constructive because otherwise "they would fight with their sticks." A committee member replied to the effect that such logic suggests that the elimination of simple assault would bring about the elimination of aggravated assault. The assault is the problem (or the professionalizing of sports and athletics in the name of winning), and this is where realistic reforms must begin.

College Administrators: Hope for the Future

In the nature of contemporary intercollegiate sports and athletics, the most viable sources and channels for meaningful reform are college administrators and more effectively organized national governing bodies (the NCAA and AIAW). As indicated in previous discussions about sports and athletics and the pursuit of education, academically sincere colleges and universities must regard student-athletes as students first and athletes second with all that this entails and requires. Sports and athletics are essential and productive in the educational process especially at the college level, but sports programs must be conducted ethically and morally with the student-athlete's academic well-being as the first priority. Such programs can and should be winning programs, but always with priorities properly ordered and with honor, decency, and integrity for the institution and for student-athletes.

College presidents and vice-presidents and other key academic administrators are primarily responsible for this, and must work to bring about a "transvaluation of values" to guarantee meaningful educational opportunity along with successful athletic participation. Earlier in this discussion about reforms in the sporting enterprise, it was contended that the ideal reform would be a reorientation of sociocultural values away from secularism and winning at all costs. The kind of responsibility assigned here to college administrators is the best hope for the realization of the beginning of this ideal. Academicians must always constitute the vanguard for the establishment and the preservation of intrinsic human values in the shaping of civilization, and at the very least they are divinely obligated to keep their own houses in order. Respected athletic figures such as John Wooden and Joe Paterno were quoted earlier saying that "the ills of intercollegiate athletics come from management" and this is where reforms must start. Many academic administrators have already picked up the gauntlet with their constructive concern about intercollegiate athletics, and others must follow if intercollegiate athletics are to serve as forces for good. The ball is in the president's court, and there is much meaning in the question "if we can't trust academicians, then whom can we trust?"

Need for National Organizations

In the practical implementation of reforms in intercollegiate sports and athletics, the academic administrators' staunchest ally is an effectively organized and properly functioning national governing body for intercollegiate sports: the NCAA and AIAW. Probably the most significant historical reform in intercollegiate sports and athletics was the creation of the NCAA in 1904 at the behest of President Theodore Roosevelt as a means of controlling violence in sports. It is important to note that the President's charge was directly to college presidents to band together and institute reforms or else submit to government control of intercollegiate sports and athletics. Thus the NCAA was originally an organization of academic administrators, and it is unfortunate that the association has drifted away from this orientation toward exclusive control by athletic administrators. In the context of contemporary abuses and corruptions in intercollegiate athletics, academic and athletic administrators would be wise to recognize the possibility of renewed threats of government intervention and control of intercollegiate sports if reforms are not effected from within. Tendencies in this direction have already been implied, beginning with government committee hearings on excessive violence in sports and athletics, antitrust situations in the sporting enterprise, and related procedural and structural anomalies in the conduct of contemporary sports participation.

The NCAA functions as the national governing body for men's intercollegiate sports programs, but currently has become the target of criticism from academic and athletic circles alleging excessive concern with financial stability and prosperity (television contracts) rather than solid leadership in more prosaic but equally important organizational concerns. Critics contend that the NCAA's machinery for enforcement of rules and regulations is relatively small and relatively ineffective, and too many instances of serious wrong-doing go undetected and unpunished. An extension of this is that the association's punitive measures for typical violations have only minimal effect and do not constitute strong deterents for misconduct by unconscionable colleges and universities. California State University (Long Beach) President Stephen Horn, long a strident voice for reform in intercollegiate athletics, asserts that:

> Too often the jockeying for power within the NCAA has reflected economic rivalry among institutions rather than a common concern for what should be the basic purpose of the organization (and of intercollegiate athletics): to assure the education of student-athletes and to protect them from exploitation—even by their own institutions.[11]

Joe Paterno, rapidly becoming one of the chief philosophical spokespersons for reform-minded athletic directors, adds that:

I believe the mood is right and the time is right for the NCAA to do something. It's a question now of whether we have the leadership. I think it's up to the NCAA to get something started. We've got a long road ahead. . . Maybe the NCAA will have to come together, throw out the rules and start over. The NCAA came together as a president's organization. Do you know how many college presidents go to an NCAA convention now? Until we get truly broad-based interest—coaches, faculty people, administrators—I think we're using Band-Aids, putting them on one place and then putting them on another.[12]

Perhaps *it is time* for history to repeat itself and have the NCAA "start all over" with or without presidential urging. And with Ronald Reagan in the White House, long associated with his dramatic portrayal of legendary sports star George Gipp (and with an honorary degree from the University of Notre Dame to seal it), the possibilities of presidential intervention are not far-fetched if such action becomes necessary. The most important force for reform within and apart from the NCAA is the active involvement and leadership of college presidents and academic administrators. Roles and values and goals must be reviewed and evaluated to guarantee the best interests of intercollegiate athletic participants as students first and athletes second, and the best interests of colleges and universities as educational communities with a mandate for academic stewardship. Little has been said in this analysis specifically about the status and role of the AIAW (the national governing body for women's athletics), and this is because the AIAW is in the throes of growth and has yet to define itself clearly in its internal structure and purposes and its relationship to the NCAA. Whether the two associations should somehow be merged or whether they should have any relationship at all is a matter of current and heated controversy, with adherents for both points of view represented in both organizations.

NCAA proponents of a merger cite this group's longer history and experience (and presumably wisdom) in intercollegiate affairs, while some AIAW members prefer a separate organization the better "to avoid the mistakes of the NCAA" in recruitment practices and athletic grant-in-aid policies and other areas of popular dispute. And still other AIAW members simply fear a total take-over by the NCAA of intercollegiate sports and athletics combining male and female participation. Recent significant developments leading toward a closer working relationship (if not a merger) include the appointment of female representatives to key NCAA committees including the prestigious Executive Counsel, and a critical legislative decision at the 1981 NCAA annual convention to permit the NCAA to sponsor and to administrate national championships in women's sports as well as men's sports. It should be noted for the record that the decision was extremely controversial in content and in parliamentary procedure, and involved an unusual hastily called second vote after the motion (to permit the NCAA to conduct women's championships) had already been defeated. Hopefully future meetings between the two associations will somehow resolve the organizational differences in the constructive interests of male and female student-athletes across the nation.

Reformation through Innovation

Another type of sports innovation sometimes heard in the context of the "great reformation" area of sports and athletics deserves only the briefest mention and commentary. This is the notion that historically popular and traditional sports (such as football, baseball, and basketball) are largely impossible to reform, and that radically new forms of sports and athletics should be devised to eliminate and avoid the abuses and corruptions of the contemporary scene. This is recommended also in the area of women's sports and athletics for related considerations—primarily the contention that females will never compete successfully with males in traditional sports, and that female versions of traditional sports will never appeal successfully to participants and spectators. The latter notion is probably debatable, although realistically women's professional basketball and softball (and abortive attempts at football) thus far have failed to generate the interest and attention originally anticipated. Women's professional golf and tennis are long established, but even here significant differences exist in purses and crowds compared to men's golf and tennis. Women's skiing and swimming and track and field probably fare somewhat better but still fall short of parity. As indicated in earlier discussions, women's intercollegiate sports and athletics have been stimulated by Title IX legislation and benefit from the natural viability of the college scene, but many such programs still endure elements of second-class citizenship in some institutions.

These projected new forms of sports and athletics are loosely defined and rather difficult to envisage. Presumably there would be movement away from emphasis on physical strength as such—for its own reward and to minimize violence and aggression for its own sake—and probably more stress on physical dexterity and agility by individuals and teams. Possibly such activities as frisbee-throwing fit the image of things to come, or perhaps dart-throwing if we can move this out of the pubs. Television sports spectaculars have unveiled other innovative attempts at new forms of sporting activities, such as male and female belly-bucking and group efforts at tilting over-sized beach balls across designated areas and sophisticated versions of tug-of-war, and even female mud-wrestling as some kind of twilight zone between sports and sex. One can only hope fervently that these will forever be recognized as the gimmicks they are, and will never be serious factors in shaping the future of the sporting enterprise. The final irony in reformation through innovation is that *agon* and *alea* (competition and chance) are fundamental human drives, and will eventually come to characterize whatever new forms of sports and athletics that might emerge. As long as scores are kept and as long as ties are not the goal of the game, participants and spectators will be concerned with winning and losing and will prefer victory rather than defeat. Competition and chance are essentially good in themselves in the context of human affairs, and true reform involves the proper control and ordering of these dimensions in the interests of winning with honor and decency and compassion. Attempts to eliminate healthy competition and fair chance will only make us all poorer in spirit and less representative of our own intrinsic nobility as symbols of freedom and lords of the universe.

Science and the Future of Sports and Athletics

These sentiments lead to the third and final area or category of predictions and speculations about the future of sports and athletics: the *cosmic* or *futuristic* complex of things to come. This is potentially the most complicated and most awesome area because it involves the most radical forms of alteration in human affairs including sports and athletics. The portent here is that we live in an age of scientific technology with significant consequences for personal recognition and creative individuality. Modern science is wondrous in its nature and its ways, and we are supremely better for its existence and its promise. The wonder and the promise are best fulfilled when science is directed to the enhancement of the human spirit in its most definitive character. Otherwise there is the strong possibility that the balance of nature will be reversed, and scientific innovations will be turned to mankind's disadvantage. There are tendencies in this direction in various aspects of contemporary society, perhaps best reflected in increasing attempts to automatize and computerize the most meaningful dimensions of our existence and our nature. Our sociocultural structure includes proclivities toward depersonalization and dehumanization: too often we lose our essential meaning through impersonal and sterile classification in social security numbers, computer print-outs, and other artifacts of technological efficiency. The philosopher Gabriel Marcel asserts pointedly that "the ills of modern society" stem from the alienation of individuality and personalism through scientific technology that dulls the human spirit.

Hopefully we will never evolve into anything like the mindless and faceless lost souls depicted in George Orwell's *1984*, but the technology exists for a scientifically regimented society with disastrous consequences for humanity including the sporting experience. An example of what could happen in sports and athletics in such a world is indicated in a popular aspect of contemporary politics, and this is the computerized prediction of election winners based on trends in relatively meagre polling returns. A futuristic application of this in sports and athletics was dramatized in a television segment featuring a match between two massive Sumo-type wrestlers. The match as such never actually occurred, since the winner was predicted by computer analysis on the basis of the slightest initial movement of the opponents toward one another. This is probably a triumph for science in the shape of things to come, but it is at best a Pyrrhic victory for the human spirit depicted so beautifully in worthy competition and struggle. It is inhuman to know the winner without experiencing the thrill of the game. The future of sports and athletics is entwined with the future of true humanism, and the dissolution of humanity as we know it is the one catastrophic development that will signal the end of the sporting enterprise. Sports and athletics best reflect mankind's passion for competition and chance, and constitute the bastion of human values beginning with freedom, courage, honesty, community, and excellence. If the sad day should ever come when automation rules society and eliminates these spiritual ideals, there will be no forum for true humanism and no forum for sports and athletics.

All this is probably speculative fantasy, but with the disturbing ring of truth and plausibility. It is within the realm of scientific technology that our sociocultural structure could evolve into a mechanical system dominated by insensitive controls directed to functional productivity. There is evidence now that our future could well involve economically based super-conglomerates organized for power and profit with little regard for human values. Perhaps we do live with the spectre of *Rollerball* as the instrument of our cataclysmic demise. If this is the divine plan for Armaggedon, then so be it. If there is the possibility for civilization's resurrection, the appropriate signs of its renaissance will be the ring of children's laughter and the sounds of play and games.

Epilogue

It is said that anything carried to its logical conclusion becomes a menacing caricature of itself. Life is larger than logic and much too real to succumb to the fantasy of caricature. Life carried to its logical conclusion is a game—the ultimate game with the world as the arena and all of us as players. The game is where life lives, the field of our triumphs and tragedies and the proving ground for our merit. In the game of life everything is sacred and nothing is sacred: we are the arbiters and we live and die by the rules we devise.

It is no wonder that sports and athletics are integral in human existence and experience. Play is the essence of our being and the reflection of our worth and transcendence. We are the envy of the universe for our capacity to know and to love, and especially for our freedom to be what we will in play and games. When Orestes opposed his god-creator Zeus and declared that he would have his own way, Zeus admonished him that he was his maker and expected submission from his subjects. Orestes replied that Zeus had made men free and now must recognize the sovereignty of human freedom.

We are created as a plaything of the gods, and our freedom to play is still the measure of our divinity. In the end three things will prevail: man's faith in the essential goodness of human nature; man's hope in the vision of the promised land; and man's love for running the good race as the symbol of our salvation.

Notes

Chapter One

1. Florence S. Frederickson, "Sports and the Cultures of Man," in *Science and Medicine of Exercise and Sports*, ed. Warren R. Johnson (New York: Harper and Row, 1969).

2. Harry Edwards, *Sociology of Sport* (Homewood, Ill.: Dorsey Press, 1973), p. 3.

3. This is the first of several lists of persons and sources cited throughout this book. These lists are intended to be representative rather than comprehensive, and are presented sometimes with a sense of literary or poetic license. Certainly additional names and works could be included according to personal preference and a desire for more extensive documentation. Most of these names and sources are readily recognizable from the annals of world literature and sports history and national media coverage.

Morgan Wootten deserves special mention in the context of the philosophical and humanistic aspects of sports and athletics. Wootten has been head basketball coach at DeMatha High School in Hyattsville, Maryland, since 1956, and has compiled a winning ratio of nearly ninety percent (677-95) against the best competition in the country. His teams have won four national high school basketball championships, five national Catholic championships, and over sixty regional and local championships. He has been the subject of national coverage in *Sports Illustrated* and *Time* and television specials, and has been enshrined with his team in the Basketball Hall of Fame.

John Wooden, himself a living legend at UCLA, comments about Wootten: "People say Morgan Wootten is the best high school basketball coach in the country. I disagree. I know of no finer coach at *any* level—high school, college, or pro. I've said it elsewhere and I'll say it here: I stand in awe of him."

More than his technical success in basketball and coaching, Wootten's most valuable contribution to sports and athletics is his philosophical and humanistic approach. He is concerned primarily with producing "good people" along with good basketball players, and impresses a rigid set of priorities on his players and teams: God, family, school, and *then* basketball. He is most proud that every member of his varsity teams (starters and nonstarters) for the past twenty years have received four-year college athletic scholarships. Co-author Bill Gilbert (with Morgan Wootten, *From Orphans to Champions*, Atheneum Press, New York, 1979) observes that ". . . He has inspired his teams and his players to heights they never dreamed possible, yet he tells them the most important achievement in life is to be a good person. He believes in building men, not just players, in preparing someone for life, not just basketball." Wootten emphasizes the same theme in his standard pre-season address to his players: ". . . If you came to DeMatha because basketball is the most important thing in your life, then you're not going to make it here because your priorities are out of order."

4. Paul Weiss, *Sport: A Philosophic Inquiry* (Carbondale: Southern Illinois University Press, 1969); Michael Novak, *The Joy of Sports* (New York: Basic Books, Inc., 1976); Earle Zeigler, *Philosophical Foundations for Physical, Health and Recreation Education* (Englewood Cliffs, NJ: Prentice-Hall, 1964); Robert G. Osterhoudt, *The Philosophy of Sport: A Collection of Original Essays* (Springfield, Ill.: Charles C. Thomas Co., 1973); Howard S. Slusher, *Man, Sport and Existence: A Critical Analysis* (Philadelphia, PA: Lea & Febiger, 1967); Harold VanderZwaag, *Toward A Philosophy of Sport* (Reading, MA: Addison-Wesley, 1972); Robert J. Higgs and Neil D. Isaacs, eds., *The Sporting Spirit* (New York: Harcourt Brace Jovanovich, 1977); James A. Michener, *Sports in America* (Greenwich, Conn., Fawcett Crest Books, 1976); Vince Lombardi, with W.C. Heinz, *Run To Daylight* (New York: Tempo Books, Grossett & Dunlap, 1963); John Wooden, with Jack Tobin, *They Call Me Coach* (Waco, Tex.: Word Books, 1973); John McPhee, *A Sense of Where Your Are: A Profile of William Warren Bradley* (New York:

Farrar, Straus and Giroux, 1965); Morgan Wootten, with Bill Gilbert, *From Orphans to Champions* (New York: Atheneum Press, 1979); Mervin D. Hyman and Gordon S. White, *Joe Paterno: Football My Way* (New York) Macmillan, 1978).

5. George Santayana, "Philosophy on the Bleachers," *Harvard Monthly*, 18, No. 5 (July 1894), 181-190; H. Graves, "A Philosophy of Sport," *Contemporary Review*, 78 (December 1900), 877-893; Elmer Berry, *The Philosophy of Athletics: Coaching and Character with the Psychology of Athletic Coaching* (New York: A. S. Barnes & Co., 1972); John Krout, *Annals of American Sport* (New Haven: Yale University Press, 1929); Peter McBride, *The Philosophy of Sport* (London: Heath Cranton, Ltd., 1932); John T. Talamini and Charles H. Page, *Sport and Society: An Anthology* (Boston: Little, Brown Co., 1973), pp. 7-14.

6. PSSS Bibliography compiled by Carolyn E. Thomas, with contributions from William Cole, Eleanor B. English, William H. Breuning, Thomas Cook, Robert G. Osterhoudt; *Journal of the Philosophy of Sport*, ed. Klaus V. Meier; published by Human Kinetics Publishers, Champaign, Illinois.

7. Historical criticism of sports and athletics began at least with the poetic admonitions of Aeschylus (525-456 B.C.).

8. Peter McIntosh, *Fair Play* (London: Heinemann, 1979), pp. 190-91.

9. Robert C. Yeager, *Seasons of Shame: The New Violence in Sports* (New York: McGraw-Hill, 1979).

10. For an excellent and topical commentary on abuses and corruptions in intercollegiate sports, see John Underwood's "The Writing is on the Wall," *Sports Illustrated* (19 May 1980), pp. 38-72.

11. Novak, *The Joy of Sports*, p. 121.

12. Leonard Shecter, *The Jocks* (New York: Paperback Library, Coronet Communications, 1969); Dave Meggyesy, *Out of Their League* (New York: Warner Books, 1971); Jack Scott, *The Athletic Revolution* (New York: The Free Press, 1971); Paul Hoch, *Rip Off the Big Game: The Exploitation of Sports by the Power Elite* (Garden City, N.Y.: Doubleday & Co., 1972); Peter Gent, *North Dallas Forty* (New York: Morrow Publishing Co., 1973).

13. Bernard Suits, *The Grasshopper: Games, Life and Utopia* (Toronto: University of Toronto Press, 1978); Johan Huizinga, *Homo Ludens: A Study of the Play Element in Culture* (Boston: Beacon Press, 1950); Roger Caillois, *Man, Play and Games* (New

York: The Free Press, 1961); Ellen W. Gerber and William J. Morgan, eds., *Sport and the Body: A Philosophical Symposium* (Philadelphia: Lea & Febiger, 1972); William A. Harper, Donna Mae Miller, Roberta Park, Elwood C. Davis, *The Philosophic Process in Physical Education* (Philadelphia: Lea & Febiger, 1977); E.F. Zeigler, M.L. Howell, M. Trekell, *Research in the History, Philosophy and International Aspects of Physical Education and Sport: Bibliographies and Techniques* (Champaign, Ill.: Stipes Publishing Co., 1971).

14. See the minutes for the 1980 PSSS annual convention in Karlsruhe, Germany.

15. For definitive discussions of sports and athletics as business ventures, see Joseph Durso, *The All-American Dollar: The Big Business of Sports* (Boston: Houghton-Mifflin, 1971); and Roger C. Noll, ed. *Government and the Sports Business* (Washington, D.C.: Brookings Institution, 1974).

16. Survey compiled by Bonnie L. Parkhouse, Department of Physical Education, University of Southern California, *Joper*, May 1978.

Chapter Two

1. Weiss, *Sport: A Philosophic Inquiry*, especially chapters I-II, pp. 3-36; also pp. 83-85; 153-55; 244-48.

2. Ibid., p. 153.

3. Ibid., pp. 23-35; 153; 176-85. Weiss proposes these answers in various forms.

4. Dr. Bruce C. Ogilvie and Dr. Thomas A. Tutko, "Sport: If You Want to Build Character Try Something Else," *Psychology Today*, 5, No. 5 (October 1971), pp. 61-63.

5. Novak, *The Joy of Sports*, pp. 142-43.

6. Gabriel Marcel, *The Mystery of Being* (Chicago: Gateway Edition, Henry Regnery Co., 1960).

7. Michener, *Sports in America*, pp. 183-217.

8. *60 Minutes*, Columbia Broadcasting System, 3 February 1980.

9. M. Marie Hart, *Sport in the Socio-Cultural Process* (Dubuque, Iowa: William C. Brown Co., 1972).

10. See "The Money Chase: What Business Schools are Doing to Us," *Time* (4 May 1981), pp. 58-69.

11. Yeager, *Seasons of Shame: The New Violence in Sports.*

12. Paul Kuntz, "What is a Philosophy of Sport," *Philosophy Today*, 20, No. 3/4 (Fall 1976), pp. 190-95. Kuntz quotes Weiss' *Philosophy in Process:* "We find in the bull-fight. . . that despite its cushioned or civilized setting, there is a transcendence of these limits in the very fact that death is being met. To meet only the demands of nature, to see what one can do with its material is one thing; to deal with her as the very locus of death. . . seems to force sport into another dimension." (*PIP,* I, p. 167)

13. The TREASURE acronym was devised by Eugene J. Fitzgerald, LaSalle College, Philadelphia, PA, in the context of his philosophy of aesthetics course. This is my own adaptation of the acronym suited to the aesthetic qualities of sports and athletics.

14. Eleanor Metheny, *Movement and Meaning* (New York: McGraw-Hill Co., 1968); Eugene Kaelin, "The Well-Played Game: Notes Toward an Aesthetics of Sport," *Quest,* 10 (May 1968), 16-28; Hilde Hein, "Performance as an Aesthetic Category," *Journal of Aesthetics and Art Criticism,* 28, No. 3 (Spring 1970), pp. 381-86; Gerber and Morgan, "Sport and Aesthetics," in *Sport and the Body: A Philosophical Symposium,* pp. 318-54; Robert G. Osterhoudt, "The Aesthetic Status of Sport," in *The Philosophy of Sport,* pp. 303-36; Ruth Casper, O.P., "Play Springs Eternal," *The New Scholasticism,* 52, No. 2 (Spring 1978), *pp. 187-201.*

In an article in the *Philadelphia Inquirer* (11 January 1978), freelance writer and poet Sandra Kohler comments on the aesthetic qualities of sports and athletics: "Sports, like art, create a universe: a humanly shaped model of the world in which we apprehend not only aesthetic but moral and ethical dimensions. The ultimate object of art—the human spirit—is revealed in the humbler games as well as the higher. . . In the ultimate sense, art too is just a game: King Lear is no more 'real' than the Stanley Cup playoffs—it is an imitation of life, not life itself. But because we see ourselves, our passions and limits and dreams and fate in both kinds of games. . . the true lover of art is never only a detached observer of aesthetic values: he is an involved participant; he is a fan."

15. Weiss, *Sport: A Philosophic Inquiry,* p. 3. An indicated in the first note for this chapter, this thesis is proposed and documented especially in chapter I-II ("Concern for Excellence" and "The Attraction of Athletics") and inter alia throughout Weiss' book. This analysis is based on these references. For a scholarly rebuttal of

Weiss' thesis see Randolph M. Feezell's "Sport: Pursuit of Bodily Excellence or Play?" in *The Modern Schoolman*, 58, No. 4, May 1981, pp. 257-270.

16. See Weiss, ibid., chapter III, "The Challenge of the Body," pp. 37-57.

17. Keith Algozin, "Man and Sport," *Philosophy Today*, 20, No. 3/4 (Fall 1976) pp. 190-95.

18. Ibid., pp. 193-94.

A somewhat related concept is the notion of *performative utterances* in routine communication and in sports and athletics. Performative utterances are statements which project an authoritative influence on one's life and actions and on the structure of (human) reality itself. Most statements and propositions in ordinary language are primarily descriptive and have little if any bearing on human existence and activity. Performative utterances are perhaps best reflected in religious commandments and legal decisions, but are clearly involved in sports and athletics as well. A good example is any sports official's declaration that a violation of the game has occurred (and the imposition of suitable penalties), or that an *out* has been made or points have been scored in a manner consistent with the progress of the game. The late Bill Klem, the legendary baseball umpire, sums it up in his reply to a base-runner who wanted to know whether he was safe or out: "You ain't nothing until I tell you what you are." See John L. Austin, *How To Do Things With Words* (New York: Oxford University Press, 1965), pp. 160ff. This reference to performative utterances was suggested by Eugene Lashchyk, philosophy department, La Salle College, Philadelphia, Pa.

19. Dr. George Sheehan, *The New York Times*, 10 November 1974. See also Dr. George Sheehan, *Running and Being* (New York: Simon & Shuster, 1978).

Chapter Three

1. This description of the characteristics of play and games is based on Roger Caillois' "The Definition of Play," in *Man, Play and Games*, pp. 3-10.

2. Bernard Suits, "The Elements of Sport," in *The Philosophy of Sport*, ed. Robert G. Osterhoudt, p. 64.

3. Scott Kretchmar, "Ontological Possibilities: Sport as Play," in *The Philosophy of Sport*, ed. Robert G. Osterhoudt, p. 76.

4. Novak, *The Joy of Sports*, pp. 122-31.

5. Bernard Suits, "What is a Game," in *Sport and the Body: A Philosophical Symposium*, ed. Gerber and Morgan, p. 12. These insights are developed at greater length in Suits' definitive work *The Grasshopper: Games, Life and Utopia* (see chapter I, note 13).

6. Roger Caillois, *Man, Play and Games*, pp. 57-58; 64; 67.

7. Roger Caillois, "The Classification of Games," in *Sport and the Body: A Philosophical Symposium*, ed. Gerber and Morgan, pp. 30-37. Page references in the following citations are from this edition.

8. Ibid., p. 31.

9. Ibid., p. 31.

10. Ibid., p. 33.

11. Ibid., p. 33.

12. Ibid., pp. 33-34.

13. Ibid., p. 35.

14. Ibid., p. 35.

15. Ibid., p. 35.

16. Ibid., p. 35; 37.

17. This schemata is an elaboration of Caillois' model in *Man, Play and Games*, p. 54 (Table II).

18. The Dionysian-Apollonian foundation for society and culture is derived from suggestions in Caillois' "An Expanded Theory of Games," in *Man, Play and Games*, pp. 71-79 and sequel.

Chapter Four

1. Jean-Paul Sartre, *Being and Nothingness*, trans. Hazel Barnes (New York: Philosophical Library, 1965); Gabriel Marcel, *The Mystery of Being* (Chicago: Gateway Edition, Henry Regnery Co., 1960); Martin Heidegger, *Existence and Being*, trans. R.F.C. Hull and Alan Crick (Chicago: Henry Regnery Co., 1949); W.C. Barrett, *Irrational Man* (New York: Doubleday Co., 1958); H.J. Blackham, *Six Existentialist Thinkers* (London: Routledge and K. Paul, Ltd., 1952); F. C. Copleston, *Existentialism and Modern Man* (Oxford: Blackfriars, 1948); Wilfrid Desan, *The Tragic Finale* (Cambridge, Mass.: Harvard University Press, 1954); Marjorie Grene, *Dreadful*

Freedom (Chicago: University of Chicago Press, 1948); Jean Wahl, *A Short History of Existentialism* (New York: Philosophical Library, 1949); Joseph C. Mihalich, *Existentialism and Thomism* (Totowa, N.J.: Littlefield, Adams Co., 1969).

2. Harper-Miller-Park-Davis, *The Philosophic Process in Physical Education,* p. 205.

3. Sartre, *Being and Nothingness*, Part 3, "Being-For-Others," especially pp. 221-360.

4. John McPhee, *A Sense of Where You Are: A Profile of William Warren Bradley* (New York: Farrar, Straus and Giroux, 1965).

5. George Harris, "Adam Smith's Invisible 'It'—An Introduction," *Psychology Today* (October 1975), pp. 45-46; excerpts from Adam Smith's "Sport is a Western Yoga, in *Powers of Mind* (New York: Random House, 1975). See also Spencer K. Wertz's "Zen, Yoga, and Sports: Eastern Philosophy for Western Athletes," in *Journal of the Philosophy of Sport*, 4, Fall 1977, pp. 68-81.

6. Smith, *Psychology Today*, p. 74.

7. Ibid., p. 48.

8. Ibid., p. 49-50.

9. Sartre, *Being and Nothingness*, p. 580.

10. Ibid., p. 581.

11. Ralph Netzky, "Playful Freedom: Sartre's Ontology Reappraised," *Philosophy Today*, 18, No. 2/4 (Summer 1974), pp. 125-36; see also Karl Jaspers, *Man in the Modern Age*, trans. Eden and Cedar Paul (New York: Doubleday Co., 1957). Jaspers is a classical existentialist philosopher who advocates seeking meaningful human freedom in play and games and sports: "Even contemporary human beings wish to express themselves in one way or another, and sport becomes a philosophy. They rise in revolt against being cabined, cribbed, confined; and they seek relief in sport, though it lacks transcendent substantiality. Still, it contains the aforesaid soaring element—unconsciously willed, though without communal content—as a defiance to the petrified present. The human body is demanding its own rights in an epoch when the apparatus is pitilessly annihilating one human being after another."

12. Friedrich Nietzsche, "Joyful Wisdom," in *The Complete Works of Friedrich Nietzsche,* ed. Oscar Levy (New York: Russell and Russell, 1964).

13. Friedrich Nietzsche, "Genealogy of Morals," in *Basic Writings of Nietzsche,* trans. Walter Kaufmann (New York: Random House,

1968); Friedrich Nietzsche, *Beyond Good and Evil*, trans. Walter Kaufmann (New York: Random House, 1966).

14. Soren Kierkegaard, *Either/Or*, trans. David Swenson and Lillian Marvin Swenson (Princeton, N.J.: Princeton University Press, 1971).

15. The descriptive language for the sports version of the stages and some of the examples are my own.

Chapter Five

1. Statement of educational/athletic philosophy by La Salle College, Philadelphia, Pa. La Salle is a private urban institution administered by the Christian Brothers (day-division enrollment 4,000). The College has conducted intercollegiate varsity sports programs for the past fifty years, and currently fields twenty-two varsity sports—eleven men's and ten women's and one coeducational (rifle). La Salle's basketball teams have been nationally competitive for decades (NCAA national champions in 1954), and have appeared in NCAA post-season competition regularly over the past several years. The women's field hockey team won the 1980 AIAW Division II national championship.

2. Dr. Thomas N. McCarthy, La Salle psychology professor and former vice president for student affairs including the College athletic program.

3. *Journal of Philosophy of Sport*, 6 (1979), p. 92.

4. Hanford letter quoted in James A. Michener's *Sports in America*, p. 280.

5. For representative statements and interpretations of regulations and recommendations, see the NCAA Manual (1979-80)—especially Bylaws on Recruiting (article 1, sections 1-9, pp. 40-51); Eligibility Rules for NCAA Championships (article 4, sections 1-7, pp. 63-77); Limitations on Financial Aid Awards (article 5, sections 1-8, pp. 78-82); and Recommended Policies and Practices for Intercollegiate Athletics (pp. 136-40).

6. Barnett Wright, *The Temple Daily News*, Temple University, Philadelphia, Pa., 30-31 October 1979. Wright's articles emphasize that student-athletes must combat academic/athletic pressures with judicious use of free time between classes and practices and other activities.

7. See the Proceedings for the NCAA National Convention, St.

Louis, January 1976. See also incisive summary statements by Richard W. Lyman, president of Stanford University, and Rev. Edmund P. Joyce, executive vice president of Notre Dame University, in *The Chronicle of Higher Education*, 13, No. 16 (20 December 1976), p. 24.

8. The issue of freshman eligibility (or ineligibility) is a matter of lasting concern among academic and athletic personnel, and aspects of the issue constituted an agenda item for the NCAA national convention in January 1981.

9. Ron Tongate, "Athletes: Counseling the Overprivileged Minority," *Personnel and Guidance Journal* (June 1978), pp. 626-29.

10. Title IX of the Education Amendments 1972: "No person in the United States shall, on the basis of sex, be excluded from participation in, be denied the benefits of, or be subjected to discrimination under any education program or activity receiving Federal financial assistance. . ." The proper interpretation and implementation of Title IX have been matters of extensive controversy over the past several years and have yet to be resolved. Much of the controversy centers on former HEW Secretary Joseph Califano's proposed guidelines published on 6 December 1978. The critical phrase in the guidelines is that colleges and universities receiving federal funds must establish "equal per capita expenditure" for male and female athletes throughout the insitution's athletic program, a prerequisite that would increase program costs by hundreds of thousands of dollars in some larger institutions. The language has since been refined to read "equal opportunity" for male and female athletes in all areas of the athletic program, but this is still subject to interpretation and clarification and has provoked litigation alleging sex discrimination in college sports in several states across the nation. The issue of Title IX legislation in women's sports seemingly has been consigned to a kind of political limbo where it might well be threatened by a calculated conspiracy of silence.

11. Novak, *The Joy of Sports*, "Of Women and Sports," pp. 191-204; Michener, *Sports in America*, "Women in Sports," pp. 155-82; Jane English, "Sex Equality in Sports," *Philosophy and Public Affairs*, 7 (1978), pp. 269-77; Weiss, *Sport: A Philosophic Inquiry*, pp. 219-29.

12. Robert T. Blackburn and Michael S. Nyikos, "College Football

and Mr. Chips: All in the Family," *Phi Delta Kappan*, 56, No. 2 (October 1974), pp. 110-13.

13. Ibid., pp. 111-12.

14. Ibid., p. 113.

Chapter Six

1. The article mentioned earlier is pertinent again here: John Underwood's "The Writing is on the Wall," *Sports Illustrated* (May 1980).

2. University of Southern California, Self-Study Report, in *The New York Times*, 19 October 1980, p. 2S.

3. Bob Hammel, "Student-Athletes: Tackling the Problem," panel discussion by John Wooden, former UCLA basketball coach; Joe Paterno, Penn State athletic director and football coach; Darrell Mudra, Eastern Illinois football coach; Nick Mannos, Skokie, Illinois, high school principal; and Bob Hammel, Bloomington, Indiana, sportswriter and panel moderator, in *Phi Delta Kappan*, 62, No. 1 (September 1980).

4. Ibid., p. 7.

5. Ibid., p. 8.

6. Ibid., p. 8.

7. Stephen Horn, "Student-Athletes: A College President Responds," *Phi Delta Kappan*, 62, No. 1 (September 1980).

8. Recorded grade reports at La Salle College, Philadelphia, Pa., for 309 student-athletes (184 males and 125 females), fall semester 1979. Statistics compiled by Rev. Raymond F. Halligan, O.P., former academic coordinator for La Salle student-athletes.

9. Quoted from *60 Minutes* report on academic/athletic abuses, CBS television documentary, 3 February 1980.

10. For an incisive and comprehensive survey of academics and student-athletes, see Stan Hochman's five-part series on Philadelphia's Big 5 basketball teams: "Hoop Dupes?" in the *Philadelphia Daily News*, Philadelphia, Pa., 25-29 February 1980.

11. University of Southern California Self-Study Report, in *The New York Times*, 19 October 1980, p. 2S.

12. Ibid..

Chapter Seven

1. For an eloquent and erudite commentary and plea to restore sanity and perspective to intercollegiate sports, see Yale President A. Bartlett Giamatti's major policy address delivered to the Association of Yale Alumni Assembly XVI, *Yale Alumni Magazine and Journal* (May 1980), pp. 13-16. President Giamatti refers to Cardinal Newman's work and supports restrictions on recruiting and post-season play.

2. Rainer Martens, ed. *Joy and Sadness in Children's Sports*, part 2, "Understanding Competition" (Champaign, Ill.: Human Kinetics Publishers, 1978), pp. 69-107.

3. Gerald Ford, "In Defense of the Competitive Urge," in *Joy and Sadness in Children's Sports*, ed. Rainer Martens, p. 72.

4. Stephen D. Ward, "Winning is Everything," in *Joy and Sadness in Children's Sports*, ed. Rainer Martens, pp. 76-77.

5. Martens, ed. *Joy and Sadness in Children's Sports*, p. 104.

6. Edward Walsh, "An American Problem: How To Live With Defeat," in *Joy and Sadness in Children's Sports*, ed. Rainer Martens, pp. 105-6.

7. Bill Bradley, "You Can't Buy Heart," *Sports Illustrated* (31 October 1977), pp. 102-114.

8. Ibid., p. 114.

Similar sentiments and attitudes about the importance of team play and team unity are expressed by Paul Westhead, former coach of the 1979-80 world champion Los Angeles Lakers professional basketball team. Westhead quotes Bradley's contention that "the dictates of community prevail over selfish personal impulses," and comments that ". . .The most important skill basketball players need to learn in order to be successful is the art of unselfishness. Our task as coaches is to direct the goals of our players from being substantially individual-centered to group-centered. . . How to instill self-sacrifice in a selfish world is no easy endeavor, but the needs and objectives of the team must be more important to the individual than his own personal gratification. . . This quality of selflessness is what many religious groups present as a way to God. By the act of being concerned for others and their well-being you find peace and fulfillment. So too by playing for the good of your team above yourself, you find the game much easier to play and to win. . . . "(Excerpted from basketball journal contributions, Paul W. Westhead, La Salle College, Philadelphia, Pa., December 1977).

9. As indicated in the final chapter of this book the trend is definitely toward all-weather facilities represented in domed and semi-domed multisport stadiums.

Chapter Eight

1. Novak, *The Joy of Sports*, p. 42.
2. Ibid., p. 40.
3. Probably some distinction should be made here with respect to the enduring values of cultural and intellectual masterworks compared to the contributions of sports and athletics. Celebrated events in the sporting enterprise may have more *immediate* impact on more segments of our society and culture, but historical triumphs in the arts and sciences have a greater dimension of lasting significance. Without reneging in the least on the premise that sports and athletics are essentially important in human existence and human experience, civilization is more likely to remember and revere Michelangelo, Beethoven, and Einstein compared to Hank Aaron, O.J. Simpson, and Gordie Howe.
4. Novak, *The Joy of Sports*, pp. 42-43.
5. Ibid., pp. 43-44.
6. Ibid., pp. 47-48.
7. This interpretation of religion and religiosity reflects contemporary theologian Paul Tillich's description of religious faith as any aspect of mankind's *ultimate concern*.

"Faith is the state of being ultimately concerned: the dynamics of faith are the dynamics of man's ultimate concern. Man, like every living being, is concerned about many things, above all those which condition his very existence, such as food and shelter. But man, in contrast to other living beings, has spiritual concerns—cognitive, aesthetic, social, political. Some of them are urgent, often extremely urgent, and each of them as well as the vital concerns can claim ultimacy for a human life or the life of a social group. If it claims ultimacy it demands the total surrender of him who accepts this claim, and it promises total fulfillment even if all other claims have to be subjected to it or rejected in its name. If a national group makes the life and growth of the nation its ultimate concern, it demands that all other concerns, economic well-being, health and life, family, aesthetic and cognitive truth, justice and humanity, be sacrificed. . . Faith is the state of being ultimately concerned. The content matters infinitely for the life of the believer, but it does not matter for the formal definition of faith. . ." Paul Tillich, *Dynamics of Faith* (New York: Harper Torchbooks, 1957), pp. 1-4.

8. Novak, *The Joy of Sports*, p. 19.

9. Ibid., p. 22.

10. Ibid., pp. 121-66.

11. Ibid., p. 46.

12. Ibid., p. 150.

13. Ibid., p. 152.

14. Ibid., p. 157.

15. Ibid., p. 158.

16. Martin Heidegger, "What is Metaphysics?" trans. by R.F.C. Hull and Alan Crick, in *Existence and Being* (Chicago: Henry Regnery Co., 1949), pp. 353-99.

17. Novak, *The Joy of Sports*, p. 159; 162.

18. Ibid., p. 145.

Chapter Nine

1. *Rollerball*, United Artists, US 1975.

2. It is interesting that the first recorded instance of sports reporting involves a celebration of the death of a hero. In the 23rd Book of the *Iliad* (ca. 750 B.C.), Homer recounts the story of "funeral games" staged by the Greek warrior-god Achilles in honor of his fallen comrade Petrocolus. The highlight of the games was a foot-race in which the winner was privileged to place the wreath on the burial site.

3. There are tentative indications in professional sports and athletics that some owners are attempting to bring about a leveling-off with respect to exorbitant salaries and bonus packages. In a convoluted and implicit way, this was one of the issues in the major league baseball players strike. National Basketball Association owners were relatively conservative in the area of salaries and bonuses for the 1980 crop of college draftees. Former Chicago White Sox owner Bill Veeck reminds everyone that "It's not the high price of stars that is expensive—it's the high price of mediocrity."

4. Michener, *Sports in America*, especially pp. 246-57.

5. Ibid., pp. 246-47.

6. Ibid., pp. 247-55.

7. Ibid., p. 255.

8. John M. Stevens, "How to Train and Educate Professional Football Players," *Phi Delta Kappan*, 62, No. 1 (September 1980), pp. 14-15.

9. Ibid., p. 14.

10. Ibid., p. 15.

11. Horn, "Student-Athletes: A College President Responds," *Phi Delta Kappan*, 62, No. 1 (September 1980), p. 13.

12. Hammel, "Student-Athletes: Tackling the Problem," *Phi Delta Kappan*, 62, No. 1 (September 1980), pp. 12-13.

Bibliography

Books

Austin, John L. *How To Do Things With Words*. New York: Oxford University Press, 1965.

Barrett, W.C. *Irrational Man*. New York: Doubleday Co., 1958.

Berry, Elmer. *The Philosophy of Athletics: Coaching and Character with the Psychology of Athletic Coaching*. New York: A.S. Barnes & Co., 1972.

Blackham, H.J. *Six Existentialist Thinkers*. London: Routledge & Kegan Paul, Ltd., 1952.

Caillois, Roger. *Man, Play and Games*. New York: The Free Press, 1961.

Copleston, F.C. *Existentialism and Modern Man*. Oxford: Blackfriars, 1948.

Davis, Elwood C.; Harper, Wm. A.; Miller, Donna Mae; and Park, Roberta. *The Philosophic Process in Physical Education*. Philadelphia: Lea & Febiger, 1977.

Desan, Wilfrid. *The Tragic Finale*. Cambridge, MA: Harvard University Press, 1954.

Durso, Joseph. *The All-American Dollar: The Big Business of Sports*. Boston: Houghton-Mifflin, 1971.

Edwards, Harry. *Sociology of Sport*. Homewood, Ill.: Dorsey Press, 1973.

Gerber, Ellen W. and Morgan, William J., eds. *Sport and the Body: A Philosophical Symposium*. Philadelphia: Lea & Febiger, 1977.

219

Gent, Peter. *North Dallas Forty.* New York: Morrow Publishing Co., 1973.

Grene, Marjorie. *Dreadful Freedom.* Chicago: University of Chicago Press, 1948.

Hart, M. Marie. *Sport in the Socio-Cultural Process.* Dubuque, Iowa: William C. Brown Co., 1972.

Heinz, W.C., and Lombardi, Vince. *Run to Daylight.* New York: Tempo Books, Grossett & Dunlap, 1963.

Higgs, Robert J., and Isaacs, Neil D., eds. *The Sporting Spirit.* Reading, MA: Addison-Wesley, 1973.

Hoch, Paul. *Rip Off the Big Game: The Exploitation of Sports by the Power Elite.* Garden City, N.Y.: Doubleday & Co., 1972.

Howell, M. L.; Trekell, M.; and Zeigler, E.F. *Research in the History, Philosophy and International Aspects of Physical Education and Sport: Bibliographies and Techniques.* Champaign, Ill.: Stipes Publishing Co., 1971.

Huizinga, Johan. *Homo Ludens: A Study of the Play Element in Culture.* Boston: Beacon Press, 1950.

Hyman, Mervin D. and White, Gordon S. *Joe Paterno: Football My Way.* New York: Macmillan, 1978.

Jaspers, Karl. *Man in the Modern Age.* Trans. Eden and Cedar Paul. New York: Doubleday Co., 1957.

Kierkegaard, Soren. *Either/Or.* Trans. David Swenson and Lillian Marvin Swenson. Princeton, N.J.: Princeton University Press, 1971.

Krout, John. *Annals of American Sport.* New Haven: Yale University Press, 1929.

Marcel, Gabriel. *The Mystery of Being.* Chicago: Gateway Edition, Henry Regnery Co., 1960.

Martens, Rainer, Ed. *Joy and Sadness in Children's Sports.* Champaign, Ill.: Human Kinetics Publishers, 1978.

Meggyesy, Dave. *Out of Their League.* New York: Warner Books, 1971.

Metheny, Eleanor. *Movement and Meaning.* New York: McGraw-Hill Co., 1968.

McBride, Peter. *The Philosophy of Sport.* London: Heath Cranton, Ltd., 1932.

McIntosh, Peter. *Fair Play*. London: Heinemann, 1979.

McPhee, John. *A Sense of Where You Are: A Profile of William Warren Bradley*. New York: Farrar, Straus and Giroux, 1965.

Michener, James A. *Sports in America*. Greenwich, Conn.: Fawcett Crest Books, 1976.

Mihalich, Joseph C. *Existentialism and Thomism*. Totowa, N.J.: Littlefield, Adams Co., 1969.

Nietzsche, Friedrich. "Joyful Wisdom." In *The Complete Works of Friedrich Nietzsche*. Trans. Walter Kaufmann. New York: Random House, 1968.

———. *Beyond Good and Evil*. Trans. Walter Kaufmann New York: Random House, 1966.

Noll, Roger C. *Government and the Sports Business*. Washington, D.C.: Brookings Institution, 1974.

Novak, Michael. *The Joy of Sports*. New York: Basic Books Inc., 1976.

Osterhoudt, Robert G. *The Philosophy of Sport: A Collection of Original Essays*. Springfield, Ill.: Charles C. Thomas Co., 1973.

Sartre, Jean-Paul. *Being and Nothingness*. Trans. Hazel Barnes New York: Philosophical Library, 1965.

Scott, Jack. *The Athletic Revolution*. New York: The Free Press, 1971.

Shecter, Leonard. *The Jocks*. New York: Paperback Library, Coronet Communications, 1969.

Sheehan, Dr. George. *Running and Being*. New York: Simon & Shuster, 1978.

Slusher, Howard S. *Man, Sport and Existence: A Critical Analysis*. Philadelphia, Lea & Febiger, 1967.

Suits, Bernard. *The Grasshopper: Games, Life and Utopia*. Toronto: University of Toronto Press, 1978.

Talamini, John T. and Page, Charles H. *Sport and Society: An Anthology*. Boston: Little, Brown Co., 1973.

Tillich, Paul. *Dynamics of Faith*. New York: Harper Torchbooks, 1957.

VanderZwagg, Harold. *Toward A Philosophy of Sport*. Reading, MA: Addison-Wesley, 1973.

Wahl, Jean. *A Short History of Existentialism.* New York: Philosophical Library, 1949.

Weiss, Paul. *Sport: A Philosophic Inquiry.* Carbondale, Ill.: Southern Illinois University Press, 1969.

Wooden, John, with Tobin, Jack. *They Call Me Coach.* Waco, Texas: Word Books, 1973.

Wooten, Morgan, with Gilbert, Bill. *From Orphans to Champions.* New York: Atheneum Press, 1979.

Yeager, Robert C. *Seasons of Shame: The New Violence in Sports.* New York: McGraw-Hill, 1979.

Zeigler, Earle. *Philosophical Foundations for Physical, Health and Recreation Education.* Englewood Cliffs, N.J.: Prentice-Hall, 1965.

Articles and Films

Algozin, Keith. "Man and Sport." *Philosophy Today* 20, no. 3/4. Fall 1976.

Blackburn, Robert T. and Nyikos, Michael S. "College Football and Mr. Chips: All in the Family." *Phi Delta Kappan* 56, No. 2. October 1974.

Bradley, Bill. "You Can't Buy Heart." *Sports Illustrated.* 31 October 1977.

Caspar, Ruth, O.P. "Play Springs Eternal." *The New Scholasticism* 52, No. 2, Spring 1981.

English, Jane. "Sex Equality in Sports." *Philosophy and Public Affairs,* 7, 1978.

Feezell, Randolph M. "Sport: Pursuit of Bodily Excellence or Play?" *The Modern Schoolman,* 58, No. 4, May 1981.

Ford, Gerald. "In Defense of the Competitive Urge." In *Joy and Sadness in Children's Sports.* Ed. Rainer Martens Champaign, Ill.: Human Kinetics Publishers, 1978.

Frederickson, Florence S. "Sports and the Cultures of Man." In *Science and Medicine of Exercise and Sports.* Ed. Warren R. Johnson New York: Harper & Row, 1969.

Giamatti, A. Bartlett. Policy address on athletics. *Yale Alumni Magazine and Journal,* May 1980.

Graves, H. "A Philosophy of Sport." *Contemporary Review*, 78, December 1900.

Hammel, Bob, and panel. "Student-Athletes: Tackling the Problem." *Phi Delta Kappan*, September 1980.

Harris, George, "Adam Smith's Invisible 'It'—An Introduction." *Psychology Today*, October 1975.

Heidegger, Martin. "What is Metaphysics?" Trans. R.F.C. Hull and Alan Crick. In *Existence and Being*. Chicago: Henry Regnery Co., 1949.

Hein, Hilde. "Performance as an Aesthetic Category." *Journal of Aesthetics and Art Criticism*, 28, No. 3, Spring 1970.

Hochman, Stan. "Hoop Dupes?" *Philadelphia Daily News*, Philadelphia, PA, 25-29 February 1980.

Horn, Stephen. "Student-Athletes: A College President Responds." *Phi Delta Kappan*, September 1980.

Kaelin, Eugene. "The Well-Played Game: Notes Toward an Aesthetics of Sports." *Quest*, 10, May 1968.

Kohler, Sandra. "Sports and the Arts are Compatible." *Philadelphia Inquirer*, Philadelphia, PA, 11 January 1978.

Kretchmar, Scott, "Ontological Possibilities: Sport as Play." in *The Philosophy of Sport: A Collection of Original Essays*. Robert G. Osterhoudt Springfield, Ill.: Charles C. Thomas Co., 1973.

Kuntz, Paul. "What is a Philosophy of Sport?" *Philosophy Today*, 20, No. 3/4, Fall 1976.

Lyman, Richard W. and Joyce, Rev. Edmund P. Debate on athletic grants-in-aid. *The Chronicle of Higher Education*, 13, No. 16, 20 December 1976.

Netzky, Ralph. "Playful Freedom: Sartre's Ontology Reappraised." *Philosophy Today*, 18, No. 2/4, Summer 1974.

Ogilvie, Dr. Bruce C. and Tutko, Dr. Thomas A. "Sport: If You Want to Build Character Try Something Else." *Psychology Today*, 5, No. 5, October 1971.

Parkhouse, Bonnie L. Survey on graduate education in sports and athletics. Department of Physical Education, University of Southern California, *Joper*, May 1978.

Rollerball. United Artists US 1975.

Santayana, George. "Philosophy on the Bleachers." *Harvard Monthly*, 18, No. 5, July 1894.

Sheehan, Dr. George. "Athletic Scholarships Yes — Academic Scholarships No." *The New York Times*, 10 November 1974.

Smith, Adam. "Sport is a Western Yoga." In *Powers of Mind* New York: Random House, 1975.

Stevens, John M. "How to Train and Educate Professional Football Players." *Phi Delta Kappan*, September 1980.

Suits, Bernard, "What is a Game?" In *Sport and the Body: A Philosophical Symposium*. Eds., Ellen W. Gerber and William J. Morgan. Philadelphia: Lea & Febiger, 1977.

———. "The Elements of Sport." In *The Philosophy of Sport: A Collection of Original Essays*. Ed Robert G. Osterhoudt Springfield, Ill.: Charles C. Thomas Co., 1973.

Tongate, Ron. "Athletes: Counseling the Overprivileged Minority." *Personnel and Guidance Journal*, June 1978.

Underwood, John. "The Writing is on the Wall." *Sports Illustrated*, 19 May 1980.

Self-Study Report. University of Southern California. *The New York Times*, 19 October 1980.

Walsh, Edward. "An American Problem: How to Live with Defeat." In *Joy and Sadness in Children's Sports*. Ed. Rainer Martens. Champaign, Ill.: Human Kinetics Publishers, 1978.

Ward, Stephen D. "Winning is Everything." In *Joy and Sadness in Children's Sports*. Ed. Rainer Martens Champaign, Ill.: Human Kinetics Publishers, 1978.

Wertz, Spencer K. "Zen, Yoga and Sports: Eastern Philosophy for Western Athletes." *Journal of the Philosophy of Sport*, 4, Fall 1977.

Westhead, Paul W. Basketball journal contributions. La Salle College, Philadelphia, PA, December 1977.

Wright, Barnett. Two-part series on academic and athletic pressures on student-athletes. *The Temple Daily News*, Philadelphia, PA, 30-31 October 1979.